COUNT ZEPPELIN
1838-1917

Zeppelin

The Story of a Great Achievement

by Harry Vissering

©2010 PERISCOPE FILM LLC
ALL RIGHTS RESERVED
ISBN #978-1-935700-36-4
WWW.PERISCOPEFILM.COM

For the great vision and unfaltering devotion to an idea that gave the rigid airship to the world, this compilation is my humble tribute to the memory of Count Zeppelin.

Harry Vissering

Chicago, August, 1922

"The forces of nature cannot be eliminated but they may be balanced one against the other."

Count Zeppelin,
Friedrichshafen, May 1914.

"THE savage can fasten only a dozen pounds on his back and swim the river. When he makes an axe, fells a tree, and builds a raft, he can carry many times a dozen pounds. As soon as he learns to rip logs into boards and build a boat, he multiplies his power a hundredfold; and when to this he adds modern sciences he can produce the monster steel leviathans that defy wind, storm and distance, and bear to the uttermost parts of the earth burdens a millionfold greater than the savage could carry across the narrow river."

—*Horace Mann*

FOREWORD

The economic value of the fast transportation of passengers, mail and express matter has been well proven. The existing high speed railway trains and ocean liners are the result of the ever increasing demand for rapid communication both on land and water.

Saving in time is the great essential. The maximum surface speed has apparently been attained. The railways and steamships of today, while indeed fast, have reached their economical limit of speed and it is not to be expected that they will be able, because of the enormous additional cost of operation involved, to attain much greater speeds.

The large Zeppelin Airship supplies the demand for a much faster, more luxurious, more comfortable and more safe long distance transportation. It is not restricted by the geographical limitations of the railway and the steamship. *A Zeppelin can go anywhere*, in fact the cruising radius of a Zeppelin is only limited by the size of the ship and the amount of fuel it can carry.

Zeppelins, only slightly larger than those actually flown during the last few months of the war, are capable of safely and quickly making a non-stop flight from Berlin to Chicago and from New York to Paris in 56 hours, carrying 100 passengers and in addition 12 tons of mail or express matter.

In November, 1917, the Zeppelin L-59 made a non-stop flight from Jambol, Bulgaria, to a point just west of Khartum in Africa and return to Jambol in 95 hours (4 days) covering a distance of 4225 miles and carrying more than 14 tons of freight besides a crew of 22, which performance remains a world's record for all kinds of aircraft, airship or aeroplane.

In July, 1919, the British Rigid Airship R-34 (copy of the Zeppelin L-33 brought down in England) crossed the Atlantic in 103 hours and after being refueled at New York returned home in 75 hours.

Count Zeppelin, Doctor Eckener and Capt. Strasser (Chief of Naval Air Service).
On the occasion of the last visit of the Count to the Airship Harbor at Nordholz.

Dr. Ing Ludwig Dürr, Chief Engineer.
Who was associated with Count Zeppelin from the start.

The German Airship Transportation Company—DELAG—(a Zeppelin subsidiary) during a period of three years just before the war, 1911-14, carried 34,228 passengers without a single injury to either passengers or crews, and after the war, from August 24th to December 1st, 1919, by means of the improved Zeppelin "Bodensee" carried 2,380 passengers, 11,000 pounds of mail (440,000 letters), and 6,600 pounds of express matter, exclusive of crews, between Friedrichshafen (Swiss frontier) and Berlin under unfavorable weather and terminal conditions, besides a flight from Berlin to Stockholm and return.

The U. S. Government has concluded arrangements (June, 1922) with the Allied Powers whereby the U. S. Navy will receive a modern Zeppelin as a part of America's share of the aerial reparations.

This new Zeppelin will embody the very latest improvements in airship design and will be delivered by being flown from Berlin across the Atlantic to the Navy's Airship Harbor at Lakehurst, New Jersey. It will be built by Luftschiffbau-Zeppelin (Zeppelin Airship Building Co., Ltd.), at their Friedrichshafen Works and will be a 70,000 cubic meter (2,400,000 cu. ft.) gas capacity commercial type, as it is intended that it will be flown in the United States to demonstrate the safety and practicability of long distance airship-transport. It will be delivered by a Zeppelin crew. The arrival in the United States of this strictly modern Zeppelin will no doubt create a wonderful interest as the American people have never seen a real Zeppelin and it will give a great impetus to airship activities throughout the world.

The U. S. Navy are building at Lakehurst, N. J., the ZR-1 modeled after the Zeppelin L-49. The ZR-1 will be of 55,000 cubic meters (1,940,000 cu. ft.) gas capacity and is intended for use as an experimental and training ship.

Luftschiffbau-Zeppelin is building (August, 1922) at Friedrichshafen a Zeppelin of 30,000 cubic meters (1,059,000 cu. ft.) gas capacity to be used for experimental and training purposes. It will be finished in the winter of 1922-23 and in time to take advantage of some of the worst of winter weather conditions for experiments having to do with airship navigation under the extremes of weather and temperature.

Considerable of the information contained in these pages has been furnished by Luftschiffbau-Zeppelin for which the author is greatly indebted to them.

HARRY VISSERING

PLATE 1

Zeppelin "LZ-1" First Ascent July 2nd, 1900.

Count Zeppelin's First Floating Shed on Lake Constance (Bodensee) and
the Zeppelin "LZ-1", July 1900.

CHAPTER I

Zeppelin and His Airships

COUNT Ferdinand von Zeppelin was born at Constance on Lake Constance (Bodensee), Germany, July 8th, 1838. His boyhood was not unlike that of others in Central Europe; and, as a matter of course, young Zeppelin was enrolled at a military school at Ludwigsburg, from which he in due time graduated into a lieutenancy in the Wurttemberg Army, but he was not particularly enthralled with the quiet life of a garrison in peace time. His creative faculties demanded something more of life than the routine of inspections, drills and dress parades. When he died on March 8, 1917, in Berlin, the whole world mourned the loss of one whose genius and vision had developed the rigid airship into a practical vehicle of the sky, proved of inestimable value in peace and war. Zeppelin had lived to see *more than a hundred rigid airships built* from his designs and under his personal supervision. And so completely was his personality interwoven with the creation of these aerial giants that throughout the world all dirigible lighter-than-air craft are looked upon as the noted Zeppelins, and are referred to as such. It is an unconscious but none the less fitting tribute to the man who, starting when he was past the half century mark, has made possible the greatest of all vehicles for us to use in our new dominion—the air.

An Officer in the American Union Army

Here in America the Civil War was attracting the adventurous from all parts of the world and shortly after it started, Zeppelin came over to join the Union Army as a volunteer officer and thus to add to his military education, but Zeppelin was not only the officer.

PLATE 2

Zeppelin "LZ-3" Over Count Zeppelin's First Floating Shed October 1906.

Zeppelin "LZ-3" in First Temporary Land Shed.
Which was erected and used while the new double shed, completed in 1908, was being
built at Friedrichshafen.

He loved to roam in out of the way places and whenever opportunity afforded he organized hunting parties and went off on long sojourns in the then sparsely inhabited regions of the Mississippi Valley. Here he played the explorer and wrote letters back home dwelling on the pleasures of exploration and the possibilities in store for him who could invent something that would take one to the far and inaccessible parts of the earth.

Zeppelin's First Rigid Design

His impressions gained during the American Civil War, where he had the opportunity of making captive balloon ascensions, and also in the Franco-German War where he had the opportunity of watching the numerous balloons leaving Paris during the siege, no doubt, first originated in Zeppelin's mind the thought of developing a large rigid airship. In fact, as early as 1873 he designed a large rigid airship, sub-divided into single compartments and he emphasized the importance of such aircraft for long distance transportation in order to help in the civilization of mankind.

In 1887 Zeppelin submitted a memorandum to the King of Wurttemberg in which he explained in detail the requirements of a really successful airship and stated many reasons why such airships ought to be large and of rigid construction. However, nothing of importance was actually accomplished until he resigned as a General in 1891 in order to give his full time to his invention.

In 1894 at the age of 56 years, with the assistance of an Engineer, Kober, he had completed the design of a rigid airship, and the modern rigid airship of today is not essentially different from Zeppelin's first design. He submitted these designs to a special committee that had been appointed by the most famous of the German scientific authorities and was greatly disappointed over the decision of the committee which, although they could not find any essential faults

PLATE 3

Zeppelin "LZ-4" Starting From the Floating Shed on a Twenty-four Hour Flight, June 1908.

Count Zeppelin's Second Floating Shed With Zeppelin "LZ-5".
Lake Constance (Bodensee) 1908.

in the Count's design, could not recommend that an airship be built in accordance with Zeppelin's plans.. Admitting that he was not the first to conceive the idea of rigid airships, Count Zeppelin, however, insisted that he had arrived at new principles and that these principles were sound. There had been several attempts to build rigids, but there always had been too much weight of the necessarily voluminous framework, which so anchored the craft with its own weight that it could not lift itself. The discovery of aluminum made this problem less difficult, however, and many models were designed with the framework of this light material.

Two years after Count Zeppelin had completed his first designs and while he was still endeavoring to arouse enough interest to warrant the construction of a rigid ship, an aluminum framework rigid ship was built by another group near Berlin. This ship was of approximately 150 feet in length, but of an essentially different design from Zeppelin's. The outer cover was made of metal. On its first trial flight it was compelled to land, due to engine trouble and the fact that the framework of the ship was not strong enough to stand the stresses of the landing, caused it to go to pieces and this failure was quickly seized upon by the then existing adversaries of the rigid airship as an argument against the construction of rigid airships with a metal framework. This was unfortunate to the cause of rigid airships, because while Zeppelin had not been identified with that attempt, all experimenters were included in the popular condemnation.

Zeppelin's improvements were beginning to be recognized and admitted, but the money necessary for the development was not forthcoming.

Financing the First Zeppelin Company

Zeppelin, in spite of many difficulties, succeeded in enlisting the necessary private capital and in 1898 organized a stock company

PLATE 4

Zeppelin "LZ-5" On an Excursion With Members of the German Parliament Aboard.
Autumn 1908.

Zeppelin "LZ-6" and "Deutschland" in the First Double Shed at Friedrichshafen.

(Aktiengesellschaft zur Foerderung-der Motorlufts-schiffahrt) to promote motor airship flights. It had a paid in capital of one million marks ($238,000).

With his characteristic sound judgment and thoroughness of purpose, Count Zeppelin chose the Lake Constance (Bodensee) country for his initial efforts. He had known the lake and local weather conditions from boyhood and was convinced that the smooth ample surface of this beautiful lake offered the best facilities for the handling, starting and landing of these extremely large craft, though it was not long before enough had been learned to alight with them on land.

Now the giant Zeppelins can land at will with perfect safety on either land or water.

Today Lake Constance is recognized as the best place in the world for the training of airship personnel.

The eyes of the entire aeronautical world were focused on the floating airship shed (Plate 1), which Count Zeppelin built and anchored in a bay close to his workshops at Manzell, near Friedrichshafen. During the months that he was making the parts in the shop and assembling his ship in the shed, there was much speculation as to its appearance. It was generally thought by others who had experimented with aircraft that Zeppelin had some very laudable ideas, but as a rule persons were skeptical concerning his ability to produce a practical machine. Interest increased and when he announced that he would fly on July 2nd, 1900, all those interested in aeronautics, who could make the trip, came to Friedrichshafen and for several days before the flight delivered professional opinions predicting failure.

The First Zeppelin Flight

They solemnly averred that the airship would bend with the weight of the gondolas under its ends. They said if it bent, the

PLATE 5

Zeppelin "Deutschland" of the "DELAG", 1910. The First Passenger Carrying Airship.

Zeppelin "Schwaben" Second Passenger Ship of the "DELAG", 1911.

engines and steering apparatus would not function. Further, they feared the ship would keel over in mid-air because, and they backed this assumption with figures and formulas based on their professional engineering knowledge and technique, as they pointed out, the center of gravity was too high. Then again the motors would surely explode the ship because the gondolas which held them were too close to the body. All expected Zeppelin to fail, and they were on hand as witnesses when first the big cigar shaped bag was floated out of its shed (Plate 1).

It was a huge thing in those days, 419.8 feet long (128 meters), with a diameter of 38.3 feet (11.7 meters). It was made up of an immense aluminum framework including 24 longitudinal girders running from nose to tail and drawn together at the ends. Joining the girders were 16 rings, (reinforced with diagonal wires), formed of transverse girders, which held the body together. On the bottom side of the body was fixed a bridge-like construction which strengthened the framework sideways and attached to it were two motor gondolas.

Over this vast framework Zeppelin had stretched an envelope of smooth cotton cloth, to lessen the friction through the air and to protect the gas bags from the direct rays of the sun. There were 16 single gas cells made of rubberized balloon cloth placed inside the framework. All were equipped with safety valves and several were provided with maneuvering valves. All together they contained 388,410 cubic feet (11,000 cubic meters) of hydrogen gas, which Zeppelin was confident would lift 24,450 pounds (12,000 kilograms).

Immediately after the ship had been floated from the hangar Zeppelin permitted it to rise off the pontoons on which it had rested and the first successful rigid airship flight was an accomplished fact. He nosed his craft up through the air, the two 16 horsepower motors sending it along slowly at 13.5 miles per hour (6 meters per second).

PLATE 6

Zeppelin "L-1". The First Naval Airship, 1912.

Zeppelin "L-2". The Second Naval Airship, 1913.

Notwithstanding this low speed the craft responded to the controls and Zepplin a few minutes later demonstrated that he could alight safely as well as take off.

The First Company Dissolved Through Lack of Funds

Zeppelin made three flights with his first airship, on the third making 17.8 miles per hour (8 meters per second) but the funds had become exhausted and overtures to the Government and industrial concerns failing, he dissolved the stock company and began anew his struggle for capital. Somehow or other people were not interested in aerial navigation. They were less willing to invest their resources in experimental machines. For five years Zeppelin labored tirelessly to make persons believe in his project. He personally traveled the length and breadth of the land endeavoring to show that this was an enterprise so stupendous in its possibilities and importance to the world that it should be substantially endorsed.

Assisted by the King of Wurttemberg

It was not until 1905 that King William of Wurttemberg having supplied the funds and an aluminum manufacturer having lent him sufficient material for another frame that Zeppelin, now 67 years old, was able to start work on his second rigid airship. He completed it that fall after working incessantly day and night, making important changes over the first design, strengthening and at the same time lightening the framework and adding considerably to the efficiency of the steering apparatus. Motors also had been developing during that period and he was able to find two 85 horsepower motors for his power plants.

And then, as the ship was being taken out of the hangar the first time, the forward steering gear was broken, and the craft was literally driven by the wind the entire length of Lake Constance, not stopping

PLATE 7

Zeppelin "L-2". Interior View showing Internal Corridor Construction.
Gas Bags Not Inflated. 1912-1913.

till it was brought up against the Swiss shore, whence with much difficulty it was returned to the workshops and repaired.

The next time he flew, Zeppelin took the ship to a height of 1640 feet (500 meters) over the lake before motor trouble developed and he was forced to land at Allgau. Though he had no assistance aside from his crew and had made no preparations the inventor was successful in landing; and he moored her there in an open field for the night while repairing the motors. Before they could be started again a winter storm swept against the craft and it was so badly damaged that Count Zeppelin with a heavy heart was forced to give orders to dismantle it.

Handicapped by Motor Trouble

There was world-wide comment over the accident which was not due to structural defect or design. Zeppelin explained that he could have survived the storm had he been able to keep his motors running. But everybody thought his dream was shattered, one more glorious failure. But Zeppelin did not agree with public sentiment. The following April he commenced his third ship, throwing into the venture his last resources along with all the enthusiasm and confidence of youth. It was this that enabled him to announce its completion in October 1906. It was exactly like the one destroyed at Allgau except for the stabilizers at the stern which had been added to permit of smooth flying (Plate 2).

Successful Trials with the Third Zeppelin

Experiments with this craft were immediately successful. Zeppelin guided it over the lake between three and four hours in a single flight, making wide circles and maneuvering under absolute control, remarkable in view of its size. The ship also showed superior speed, making 28.8 miles per hour (13 meters per second).

PLATE 8

Zeppelin "L-3" Naval Airship, 1914.

Zeppelin "L-11" Naval Airship, 1915.

This ship brought Zeppelin and his assistants their first public recognition. The German Government offered the inventor a new floating shed (Plate 3), larger than the old one, which would enable him to improve his craft and enlarge them. To him this was the most essential. He more than any other apparently realized that he must increase their size to develop practical weight lifting capacity.

The Government Becomes Interested

Meanwhile he continued his demonstration flights with his third ship, culminating on October 1st, 1907, in a brilliant 8 hour flight of more than 218.5 miles (350 kilometers). Thereupon the Government officials declared their willingness to take over Count Zeppelin's ships if they fulfilled certain requirements, among them a twenty-four hour flight. Early the next summer Zeppelin took out another new ship, LZ-4 (Plate 3), somewhat larger than its predecessors, holding 529,650 cubic feet (15,000 cubic metres) of hydrogen. This increased size gave it a carrying capacity of 37,478 pounds (17,000 kilograms) which, with increased motor power—each engine estimated at approximately 100 horsepower—made it a practical weight carrying and speedy craft. Count Zeppelin with an eye to the passenger and military possibilities had also built into the forward part of the hull, on top, an observation platform. It marked the beginning of refinement in design and conveniences which has been continued unceasingly. Here was an airship which Zeppelin felt worthy of demonstrating to the public at large.

Zeppelins for Commerce and War

His great flight on July 1st, 1908, was as successful as it surely was daring for he took the new rigid up over the Swiss Alps to Lucerne and back again.

The world was astounded, particularly his contemporaries, a majority of whom unhesitatingly flooded the grand old man with

PLATE 9

Zeppelin "L-13" Naval Airship Leaving Friedrichshafen for Its North Sea Base, 1915.

Zeppelin "L-30" Naval Airship, 1916.

enthusiastic messages of congratulation. Just as he had worked so devotedly to bringing forth something in which the German people could have faith, so was his faith justified. The public was wildly enthusiastic. Everybody was proud of the accomplishment on German soil and joyfully acclaimed Zeppelin whose lone ideas were now the ideas of a nation. His triumph was not only official but national. His vision was the vision of the people and it was an accomplished fact.

Rarely had there been such national interest shown in any sort of venture as that represented by the vast throngs that gathered from all parts of the empire to witness the start of the official duration flight on August 4th that year. Zeppelin planned to sail the ship down the Rhine Valley toward Mainz and return. He got away on schedule and disappeared in the soft haze, all Germany receiving reports of his progress as the ship appeared for a few moments over a village and then out of sight once more.

But disaster awaited the gallant ship. On the return flight motor trouble caused a forced landing at Echterdingen near Stuttgart. A storm blew up and the airship was torn from its moorings. As it was being whirled into the air, the entire structure was suddenly enveloped in a solid flame and Zeppelin a few moments later was gazing at the twisted skeleton of his latest efforts.

The Zeppelin Endowment

It was thought then that Zeppelin had built his last airship. He had employed all his own personal resources in that venture, and though the rigid had performed remarkably, even his closest friends could see nothing but failure in further attempts to establish the new science. But they were wrong. Zeppelin had been more successful than he realized. His persistent efforts had continuously improved the rigid type. Each flight was better and more efficient than the

PLATE 10

Zeppelin "L-43" Naval Airship, 1917. Showing Maybach Motor Works and Part of Friedrichshafen.

Zeppelin "LZ-77" Army Airship, 1915.

ones preceding it. All this had been noted by the people. When it was learned that Count Zeppelin had no funds with which to continue, a popular subscription campaign was started in various sections, with the result that within a few weeks 6,000,000 marks (approximately $1,500,000) had been contributed and turned over to Zeppelin for him to use as he saw fit in carrying on his experiments. Here indeed was recognition. For the money had come from persons of high and low degree, from huts and palaces. The Zeppelin fund was truly representative of the people. It made the shops and hangar on Lake Constance a popular institution. For the first time in his life the inventor found his airship enterprise on a firm financial basis. With this foundation he was able to increase his shop and laboratory facilities and make important changes in his organization. Instead of being forced to produce something for demonstration flights alone, he was able to concentrate on practical development. His personnel was ably qualified for the new work. Many of his assistants had been with him since the beginning. His progress had been theirs in the new science of lighter-than-air engineering. Many of these men are still with the Zeppelin organization which retains the original name created by the popular support of the German people.

The Beginning of the Zeppelin Organization

With the 6,000,000 marks presented to him Count Zeppelin founded the "Zeppelinstiftung zur Foerderung der Luftfahrt" (Zeppelin Endowment for the Propogation of Air Navigation). This organization is the exclusive shareholder of Luftschiffbau Zeppelin (the constructing company), and through this controls the many subsidiary companies, each one producing essential parts of the Zeppelin so that the entire organization is practically independent of outside sources. The various organizations have been added to and

PLATE 11

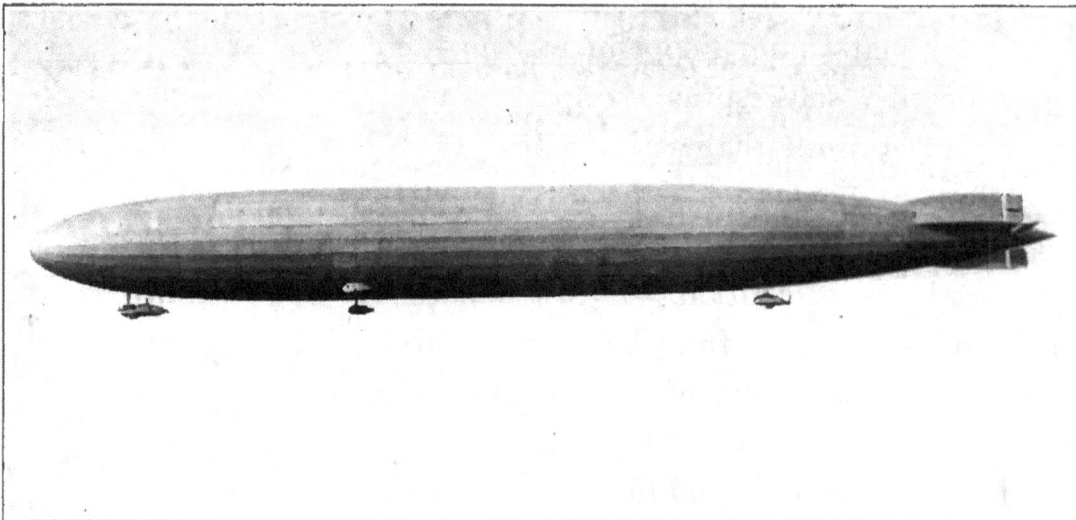

Zeppelin "L-59" Naval Airship.
Which made the still unbroken World's Record Non-Stop Flight of 4225 miles from Jambol in
Bulgaria to just west of Khartum in Africa and back to Jambol, carrying
14 tons of freight in 95 hours, November, 1917.

Zeppelin "L-59" Engine.
Telegraphs and Navigators Desk.

Zeppelin "L-59" Elevator Rudders Control
Stand and Altitude Navigation Instruments.

developed at intervals since the Zeppelin Endowment was created in 1908. They are not only concerned with producing airships and all their parts but with developing airplanes, seaplanes and power plants, with the special machinery so important to the success of the new aircraft which Zeppelin continuously produced and which proved superior to other products, due in no small part to the splendid organization developed by means of the popular fund, the profits from which under the terms by which Count Zeppelin accepted it, must continuously be thrown back into the treasury "to be used exclusively for the propogation and development of air navigation."

When Count Zeppelin died in 1917 his assistants were placed under obligations to carry on the work and administer the Zeppelin Endowment according to the original terms which do not limit its activities to national boundaries, but encourage the development of aerial navigation throughout the world.

Early Development and Flights

Commencing in 1908 Zeppelin devoted his energies to perfecting aircraft. There were many epoch making achievements, not only the record flights and increasing efficiency and performance tests but continuous discoveries and inventions no less important and significant because they were for the time being accomplished within the walls of laboratory and factory. They constitute one of the most remarkable chapters in this age of mechanics and engineering, and are worthy of further explanation later on.

One of the first flights, under the new organization, was that of the new Zeppelin Z-1, April 1st, 1909, from Lake Constance to Munich. Before it could land at Munich a heavy southwest wind pushed it back from the field over which it hovered. The Commander decided to "weather the storm" in the air; and for the first time in the history of aerial navigation the airship remained aloft,

PLATE 12

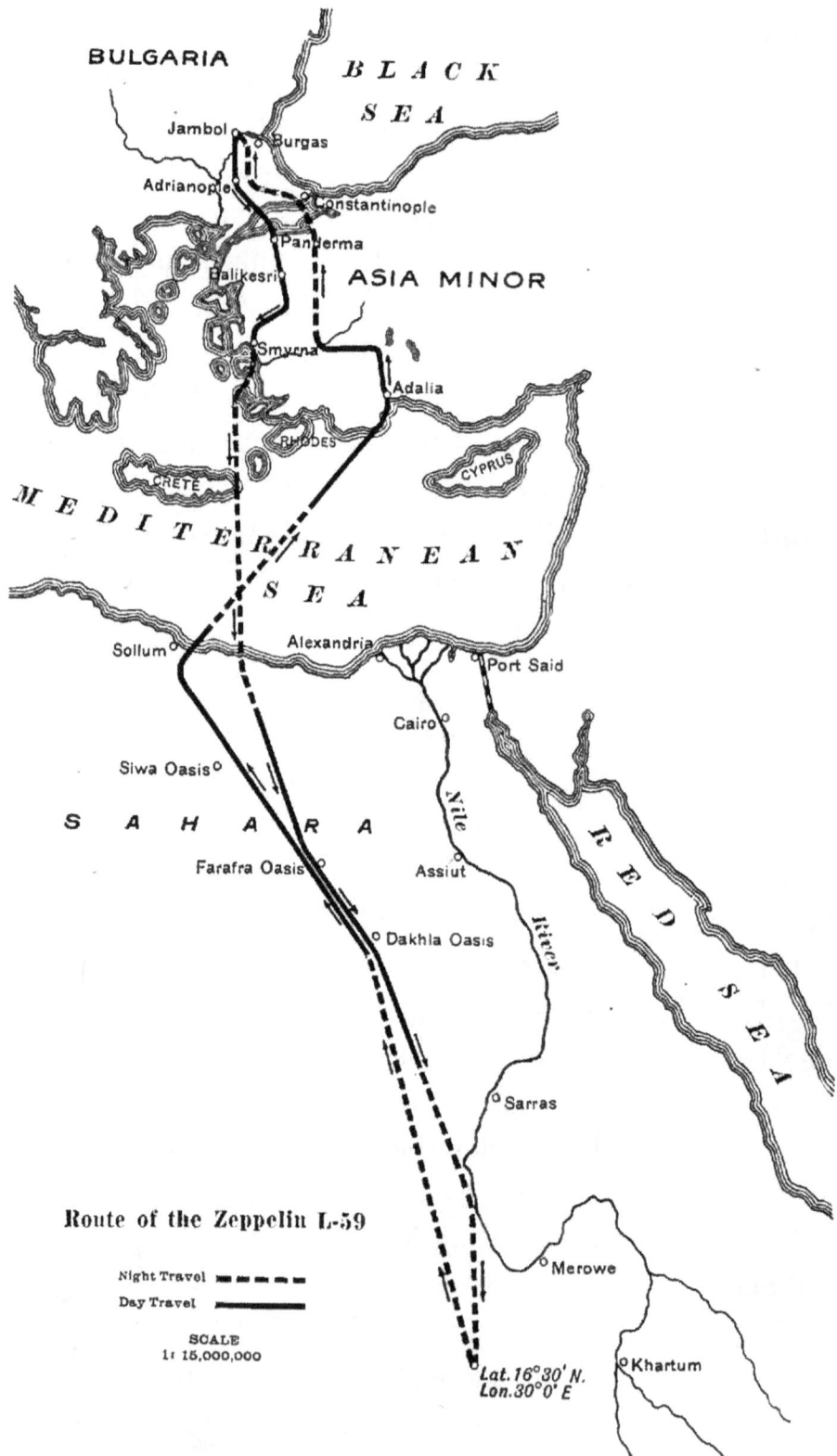

BULGARIA

BLACK
SEA

Jambol○   ○Burgas

Adrianople

Constantinople

Panderma

Balikesri   ASIA MINOR

Smyrna

Adalia

RHODES

CYPRUS

M E D I T E R R A N E A N
S E A

CRETE

Sollum○   Alexandria   ○Port Said

Cairo○

Siwa Oasis○   Nile   R E D   S E A

S A H A R A

Farafra Oasis○   Assiut○

○Dakhla Oasis   River

○Sarras

Route of the Zeppelin L-59

Night Travel ▬ ▬ ▬
Day Travel ▬▬▬

SCALE
1: 15,000,000

○Merowe

Lat. 16°30' N.
Lon. 30°0' E   ○Khartum

her nose against the wind, her motors turning over just enough to keep her in the same spot. Eleven hours later the Z-1 was still up but shortly afterward signalled that she was being forced to land because her fuel supply was becoming exhausted. Soldiers detailed for the purpose assisted in mooring her fast in a field near Loiching, where guarded by hundreds she lay all night in the storm, unharmed, though repeatedly assailed by squalls which often swept against her with 40 miles per hour (18 meters per second) velocity. The next day she went up and hopped over to Munich and received a wildly enthusiastic greeting from the thousands who had followed her adventure with personal pride and interest. The Z-1 spent four hours flying over Munich and then turned on her heels and back to her harbor at Friedrichshafen. If there was anything necessary to silence the few critics who still entertained doubts as to the ultimate practicability of rigid airships, that flight of the Z-1 accomplished the purpose.

Count Zeppelin meanwhile was rebuilding his "Echterdingen" airship and on May 29th, 1909, he took it out of Manzell toward the north of Germany. He kept on until he reached Bitterfeld before turning back toward Lake Constance. After 38 hours in the air during which he had traversed 683.5 miles (1100 kilometers) he landed at Goppingen for gasoline. In landing the ship struck a tree but the damage was quickly repaired and the rigid was able to return under its own power to the air harbor on Lake Constance.

Hailed as National Hero

After a thorough overhauling Count Zeppelin flew the same airship to Berlin, at the express invitation of the Kaiser, who gave a dinner in his honor at the Royal Palace following an enthusiastic popular reception from the entire populace in the capitol. On his return to Lake Constance he met severe storms and a broken pro-

PLATE 13

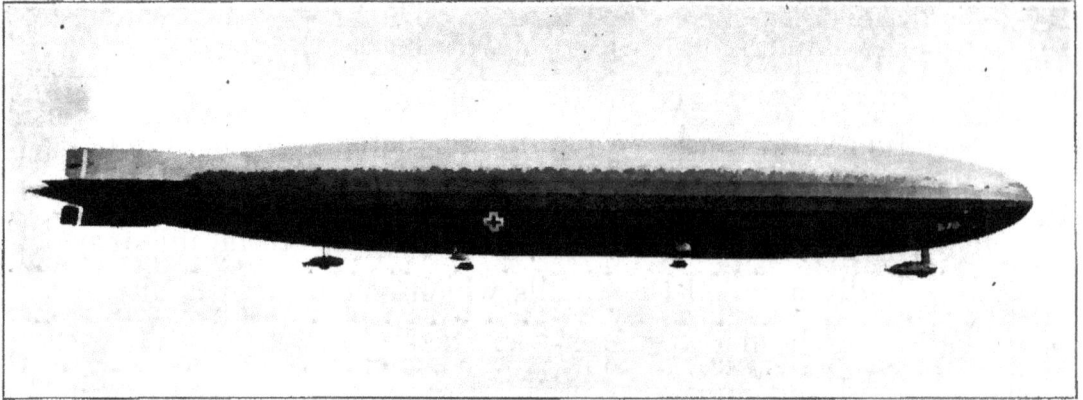

Zeppelin "L-70" Naval Airship, 1918.
The fastest of the "big ones" with a speed of 82 miles per hour.

Zeppelin "L-71". The Last Naval Airship in Actual Service.
Leaving Friedrichshafen, 1918.

peller compelled a landing. It was found that a piece of the blade had penetrated one of the gas bags; and three days were required to repair the damage. Finally, after 27 hours in the air, the ship once more rested in its home shed. It is said that this flight forever established Zeppelin in the confidence of the people and the Government. His ships acquired the reputation of the builder in being able to surmount tremendous difficulties. The Zeppelin headquarters at Friedrichshafen became the German Mecca. But the Germans were not alone in their pilgrimage for thousands of persons interested in aeronautics journeyed to Lake Constance on the shores of which great plants had grown up on the land which Zeppelin had purchased for his wonder city of the air.

In the fall of 1908 the members of the Reichstag and the Bundersrath came to Friedrichshafen, a hundred or more trusting themselves to the Zeppelin ship, the sole feature of the national celebration. Thousands of watercraft dotted the clear waters of the lake as the Zeppelin went up again and again filled to capacity with the leaders of German political, financial, and industrial life (Plate 4). Zeppelin was hailed as a national hero, and more, for it was generally recognized that his great vehicles possessing such speed and durability were world travelers and as such would do much toward bringing all parts of the world together and thereby eliminating national borders—as far as trade, travel, and commerce were concerned, at least.

The New Construction Plant

It was during the same year that Zeppelin abandoned the floating shed at Manzell, where all his ships had been built. New work shops were located on shore near Friedrichshafen (Plate 4). Half of the original contribution went into the new construction plant which was incorporated as Luftschiffban-Zeppelin, G.M.B.H. (the Zeppelin Air-

PLATE 14

Zeppelin "L-70" Naval Airship Entering Largest Shed at Friedrichshafen.
Winter of 1918.

ship Building Co., Ltd.). Here the construction of the new Zeppelins was begun with augmented forces of engineers and workmen.

Naturally the first airship was ordered by the Deutsche Luftschiffahrt A. G. ("DELAG")—the German Airship Transportation Company—which had a paid in capital of 3,000,000 marks ($714,-000.00) subscribed by a number of public spirited men solely to start a Zeppelin passenger and mail service. It was planned to employ larger ships than those with which Zeppelin had convinced the public, to secure greater lifting and carrying capacity. These ships developed rapidly.

Military Value Proved by Commercial Operation

They attracted attention among the military authorities who had decided that the Zeppelins offered advantages over the existing types of observation aircraft, that they were in no way difficult to handle in the air or on the ground and, in fact, were better adapted to military purposes than others previously built. A deciding factor in favor of the Zeppelins was the ease with which they could be put into their sheds after each flight. The Government, accordingly, ordered three airships built and equipped for military service. Their performance was kept secret but they were accepted and obviously performed equally as well as their contemporary commercial craft.

There was the Zeppelin **"Sachsen"** which flew to Vienna from Baden-Baden in less than eight hours. This commercial flight led the German army to buy three more military ships of the **"Sachsen"** type.

Activities Early in the War

The Navy followed suit and in October, 1912, bought the L-1 (Plate 6), for experimental and training purposes in connection with the fleet. The L-1 carried 706,200 cubic feet (20,000 cubic meters) of Hydrogen and proved its worth on its trial flight from Friedrich-

PLATE 15

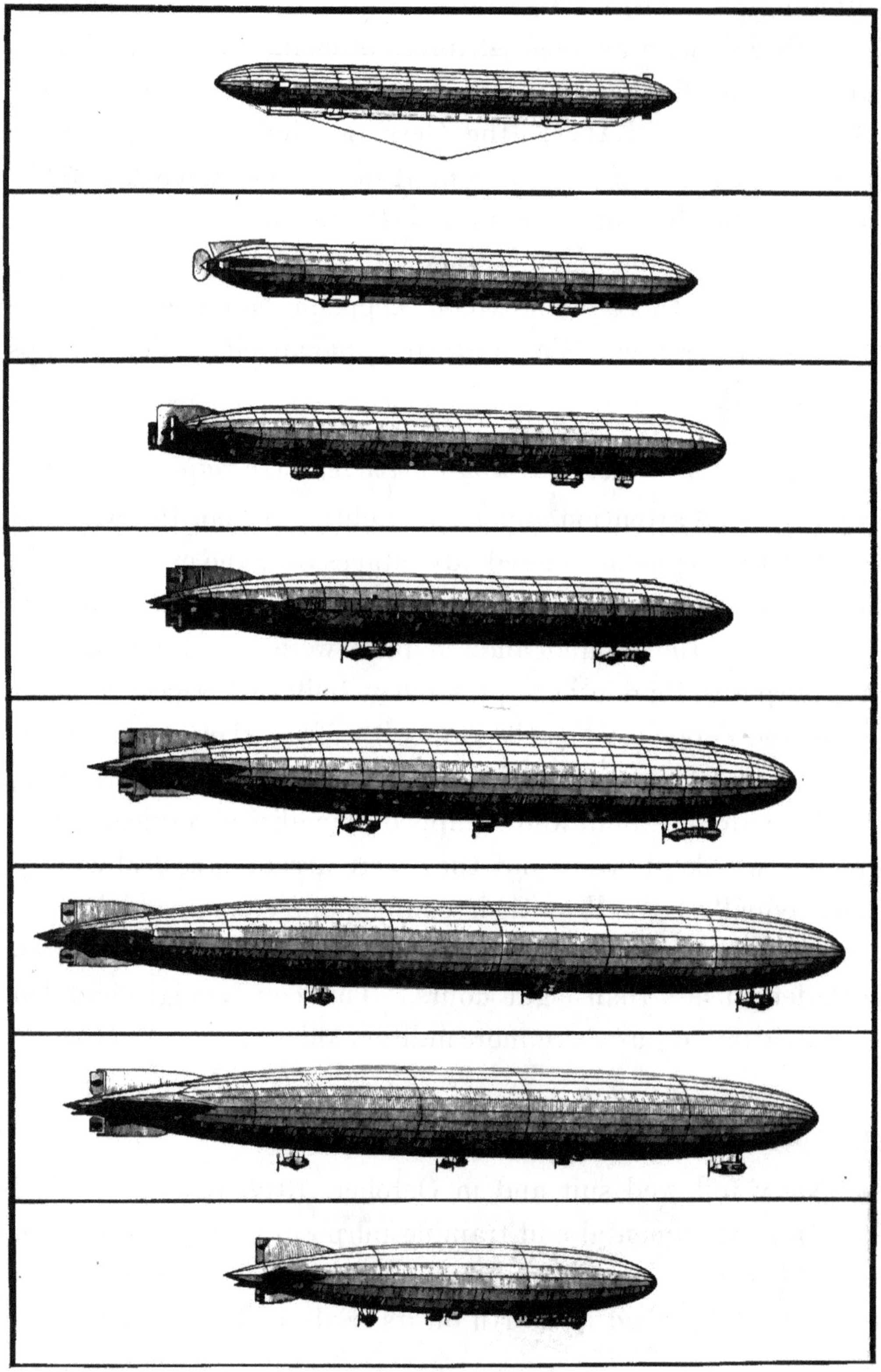

Year		Builders Designation
1900		LZ-1
1908		LZ-5
1913		LZ-18
1915		LZ-40
1916		LZ-62
1917		LZ-104 African Ship
1918		LZ-113 Last of War Types
1919		LZ-120 "Bodensee" and "Nordstern"

Development of the Zeppelin from 1900 to 1919.

shafen, thence north over Germany to Helgoland in the North Sea, thence to the Baltic, side trips here and there, and finally to the airship harbor at Johannisthal where it was to be stationed. The flight lasted 34 hours.

This persuaded the Naval officials that Zeppelins were essential in marine warfare both for offense and defense. Another order was placed, this time for a Zeppelin of much larger dimensions. It was christened the L-2 and delivered in September, 1913 (Plate 6). This ship represented an utterly new departure in design, later universally adopted. A corridor was built forming a keel on the inside and bottom of the ship (Plate 7). It had a gas capacity of 953,370 cubic feet (27,000 cubic meters) and was equipped with four motors of 180 horsepower each.

Being the first of the kind it was inevitable that the corridor arrangement should develop a flaw. It lacked proper ventilation. Hydrogen leaked out from the ship and was drawn into the motor gondolas. On one of its first flights this caused an explosion on the L-2 which sent it to the ground a wreck.

Operations with the Fleet

Early in the spring of 1914 another Zeppelin, the L-3 (Plate 8) was delivered. It held 787,400 cubic feet (22,300 cubic meters) of hydrogen and carried besides its own weight approximately 19,840 pounds (9,000 kilograms). The average speed was 43.5 (70 kilometers) per hour with motors aggregating 630 horsepower. It carried at least 6,614 pounds (3,000 kilograms) to a height of 9,186 feet (2,800 meters). The L-3 was the only naval airship Germany possessed at the beginning of the war.

Following the ideas of the inventor both the German army and navy used the Zeppelins for strategical reconnoissance in the early days of the conflict. The Zeppelins flew the western and eastern

PLATE 16

Zeppelin Airship Bldg. Co.'s Plant, Friedrichshafen, 1910.
Showing First Double Shed (now used for Hull Frame Work only) Machine Shops, Foundries and Office Buildings.

Zeppelin Airship Bldg. Co.'s Plant, Friedrichshafen, 1919.
Note the two large single sheds. The largest shed is 115 feet high, 151 feet wide and 787 feet long.

boundaries of the empire seeking information concerning the movements of the Allied armies. This proved dangerous, however, for the airships then could not rise to high altitudes; and consequently were exposed to enemy fire from the batteries below and airplanes above.

The L-3 operated with the fleet in the North Sea and her activities served to show the value of supplying as quickly as possible Zeppelins able to fly high and with greater speed than ever. It was also found advisable to cease flying over land by day. The Zeppelins became the night cruisers of the air, and were assigned the task of destroying railway junctions, bridges and ammunition dumps along the enemy line of advance.

The Navy soon acquired the Zeppelins L-4, L-5, L-6 and L-7, which joined the L-3 in the North Sea operations where they became indispensable as the eyes of the fleet and a continual menace to the enemy attempting to establish himself on the German Coast. All these airships were duplicates of the L-3 except in minor details. Their hulls long and cylindrical, of uniform cross sections, that is excepting the ends each part was the same size as the others. This was the first attempt at standard construction and it permitted quantity production more economical and quicker for they were not compelled to design and fabricate each section as it was needed. The plant at Friedrichshafen had been expanded and was working to capacity. Every effort was made to save time. The result was remarkable for they were able to produce one Zeppelin every six weeks. Late in 1914 the Zeppelin Z-11 was delivered to the army and the L-8 to the navy.

The Growth of the Zeppelins

Larger sheds (Plates 8 and 9) were completed at Friedrichshafen enabling Zeppelin to build bigger ships which could give the performances he felt was essential.

PLATE 17

Zeppelin Airship Bldg. Co.'s Colossal Plant at Staaken (1919). Near Berlin.
Consisting of two large sheds (at the left) between which is located the Traverse Ring Fabrication Shed. The Administration Bldg. is shown in the right foreground.

Zeppelin Airship Bldg. Co.'s Staaken Plant. (View taken from a Zeppelin).
By far the largest and most complete airship building plant in the world.

The first of these, the LZ-38, left the shed in April, 1915, and joined the army. It had 1,130,000 cubic feet (32,000 cubic meters) of hydrogen capacity and was fuller, that is, its ratio of length to diameter was 9 to 1 where in the former ships it was 11 to 1. The wider girth afforded more freedom in design and the stern was drawn out much finer, resulting in more speed; on later ships reaching 58.1 miles per hour (26 meters per second). The LZ-38 could carry a useful load of 30,865 pounds (14,000 kilograms) besides her own weight, more than 37% of her total lift. The Zeppelins of this type (Plate 10-LZ-77) proved from the day they were first flown equal to all the demands made upon them.

North Sea Patrol Flights

They cruised over the North Sea scouting and guarding the coastline, remaining in the air for thirty hours at a time. They flew out from the western outlet of the Kiel Canal, northward along the shores of Denmark to the Norwegian coast and thus were able virtually to command the sea hundreds of miles around with powerful glasses.

One day when the true details of the Skagerrak Naval Battle are given to the world, it will realize the vital part which the Zeppelins played. They consistently hampered the enemy's mine laying operations and rendered timely and valuable support to the counter-actions of the fleet. In discovering mines they were particularly effective; and this work alone, about which the world was uninformed, justified fully the time and labor put into their construction.

Ten Zeppelins of the L-38 type were delivered to the navy in 1915, numbered from L-10 to L-19 inclusively. Approximately as many were turned over to the army during the year, each one being slightly improved. Zeppelin and his staff of experts were always

PLATE 18

The Maybach Motor Works, 1916.
Practically all of the Airship motors were made in this plant.

Zahnradfabrik Friedrichshafen, G.m.b.H., 1915. (The Cogwheel and Gear Works).
Part of Friedrichshafen and Lake Constance in the background.

able to profit by the practical experience which the ships were undergoing almost daily.

Zeppelins Become Lighter and Stronger

The hulls were strengthened and made more rigid, yet lighter, machine guns were mounted at proper points of vantage and bomb dropping apparatus so perfected that heavy loads of explosives could be carried in absolute safety, yet instantly released and with remarkable accuracy. An observation car was added to each new ship.

The Zeppelin Observation Car

This car was one of the most unique inventions developed during the war. It could be lowered with an observer aboard, fully one kilometer (3,280 feet) below the Zeppelin. Here the observer could get his bearings while his ship lay far above hidden in the clouds. The ship could fly or drift above the clouds to a point directly over the spot to be bombed, then by lowering the car with the observer through and just below the clouds, he was able to direct both the operations of the ship and the bombing. A telephone connection ran up through the supporting cable. He was able to signal for bomb releases and navigate so efficiently that any objective could be attacked without danger of the enemy seeing the Zeppelin lurking behind the clouds.

Another Zeppelin, the L-20 was delivered to the navy early in 1916. It had hydrogen capacity of 1,271,160 cubic feet (36,000 cubic meters) though the diameter was the same as the others. The L-20 carried a useful load of 37,478 pounds (17,000 kilograms), and an increase of 1,312 feet (400 meters) over their ceiling and made the same speed with the same horsepower.

During the year Zeppelin delivered seven more ships of this type, but possessing greater efficiency. The navy received five of them and the army two.

PLATE 19

Maybach Airship Motor of 145 Horsepower, 1911.

Maybach Airship Motor of 180 Horsepower, 1913.

Anti-Aircraft Defenses Compel Zeppelins to Fly Higher

The Allies meanwhile had developed anti-aircraft defenses and their airplanes possessed greater climbing ability. To meet these new conditions the airships were continuously compelled to fly higher. They also required speed greater than the average of 54 miles per hour (25 meters per second) because while navigating over the North Sea they frequently encountered winds of from 33.5 to 40 miles per hour (15 to 18 meters per second).

To meet these conditions the L-30 was built (Plate 9). It had a gas capacity of 1,942,000 cubic feet (55,000 cubic meters) and was nearly twice as large as the original 1,129,920 cubic feet (32,000 cubic meters) four motored ships. The L-30 was ready in May, 1916. It was almost perfectly streamlined. The long cylindrical hull, so convenient from a production standpoint, had been abandoned. The L-30's stern tapered gracefully to a fine point. It was driven by six 240 horsepower Maybach motors, arranged practically as before. One was located in the forward gondola with a direct drive propeller, another three motors in the rear gondola, one with a direct drive and two others each in a separate gondola located opposite each other on the sides of the hull amidships, so as not to interfere with the efficiency of the propeller in the rear gondola. The L-30 carried 63,933 pounds (29,000 kilograms), about 45% of its total lift. Other Zeppelins of her class had a useful lift of 50% due to better design and superior materials. This represented a marked advance, as the preceding types lifted only 37% of their weight. The ceiling had been increased, too, by more than 3,280 feet (1,000 meters). They could now ascend from 11,800 to 14,750 feet (3,600 to 4,500 meters), depending on the load and weather conditions. They made a speed of 63 miles per hour (28 meters per second).

PLATE 20

Maybach Airship Motor Type HSLu of 240 Horsepower, 1915.

Maybach Airship and Aeroplane Motor Type Mb4a of 260 Horsepower at an Altitude of 10,000 Feet, 1918.

Faster Zeppelins for Scouting

These Zeppelins proved exceedingly valuable for scouting. They were flown in all kinds of wind and weather. So great was their capacity for fuel that there was no task too great for them to undertake. But then, airplanes were constantly being improved, and they could rise quickly to high altitudes. The planes carried machine guns firing phosphorous incendiary bullets fatal to the hydrogen filled hull of the Zeppelins if overtaken. Airplanes, naturally, could outdistance airships, and there was no escaping them. The Zeppelins were compelled to fly still higher than the L-30 type. There shortly appeared other Zeppelins carrying loads of more than 39 tons or 60% of the total lift of the ship; and they could fly at an altitude of 19,684 feet (6,000 meters) with 13,228 or 15,432 pounds (6,000 or 7,000 kilograms), without depending on the thrust from the motors.

In the fall of 1917 "altitude" motors were developed, larger and having supercompression. They did not develop full power at sea level but instead functioned normally at 10,000 feet altitude above sea level. They, moreover, gave ample power higher than that. They speeded up the Zeppelins to 70.5 miles per hour (31.5 meters per second).

The Zeppelin company built thirty-six ships of this type (Plate 10-L43), from 1916 to 1918; and they were used by the army and navy. The British R-34, which crossed the Atlantic in 1919, was an exact duplicate of the Zeppelin L-30 type.

Zeppelin Vision of World Transport

Count Zeppelin was working on his post-war plans for commercial aerial transport when he died in March, 1917. His latest ships had demonstrated their worth as cargo carriers, not only in war but in peace. Before hostilities commenced he had seen thousands of passengers carried in his Zeppelins. An account of these operations will be found in Chapter III.

PLATE 21

Zeppelin Giant Seaplane Built at Potsdam Plant, 1917.

Zeppelin-Dornier Twin (Tandem) Motored All Metal Commercial Flying Boat, 1919.

His Will Carried Out After His Death

They had justified the inventor's faith and inspiration. He had never abandoned his ideas of world transportation and was completing a survey of requirements and conditions to be met when, during a flight, he contracted inflammation of the lungs. Though mortally ill and old in years—he was seventy-eight—Count Zeppelin held conferences in his sick chamber, passing on to his assistants the big idea of airship transportation. They have since continued the work where Count Zeppelin left it. Following the funeral at Stuttgart airships dropped garlands and wreaths of flowers on his grave, in honor of the man who had done so much and had perfected an organization capable of performing the tasks remaining.

The Record Flight of L-59

There is ample proof of what a modern Zeppelin can accomplish when commercially operated and not forced to operate at the highest possible altitude and maintain maximum speed. In November, 1917, the Zeppelin L-59 (Plate 11) was sent to German East Africa with medicines and ammunition for the beleaguered colonial troops. The Zeppelin was especially prepared for the flight, all superfluous equipment, such as bomb dropping apparatus and armament being removed, all available space reserved for the cargo. The L-59 was longer by 98.5 feet (30 meters) than the others. This made room for two additional gas bags. Inside her 744½ foot hull (227 meters) were 2,381,000 cubic feet (68,000 cubic meters) of hydrogen. She could carry 50 tons easily. With only five motors she averaged 62.6 miles per hour (28 meters per second).

Flown from Germany to Jambol in Southern Bulgaria, the L-59 was there loaded with 9 tons of machine gun ammunition and 4 tons of medical supplies and with 21 tons of gasoline for the motors.

PLATE 22

Zeppelin-Dornier All Metal Flying Boat Type DoRs III, 1918.

Zeppelin-Dornier All Metal Flying Boat Type DoRs IV, 1918.

4225 Miles in Less than Four Days

The great Zeppelin sailed out of Jambol (Plate 12) at 9 o'clock in the morning, crossing northwestern Asia Minor, then the Aegian Sea, south of Smyrna and on between the Islands of Crete and Rhodes and across the Mediterranean, reaching the African Coast by daybreak the next day.

The great Sahara Desert was then crossed, the L-59 passing over the oasis of Farafrah and then Dakhla. Military headquarters at Berlin, meanwhile, were trying to reach the Zeppelin by wireless. The German Intelligence Office had intercepted a British wireless message to the effect that the Colonial troops had surrendered to the British. The L-59 had passed through a severe storm the night before and had taken in her radio antenna; and it was not until she was over Djebel Ain, west of Khartum that she listened in and picked up the message. In a day and a half the L-59 had traversed 1865 miles (3,000 kilometers). Without stopping the Zeppelin was turned about; and after retracing its path across the Sahara, thence over the Mediterranean to Adalia on the coast of Asia Minor, and flying high over Asia Minor and the Black Sea, arrived back in Jambol in less than four days from the time it set out from that port. There remained sufficient fuel aboard for two or three days additional flying. The ship, under the same conditions, could have flown from Hamburg to Khartum and return. As it was she traveled 4,225 miles (6,800 kilometers) on a non-stop flight which, though it occurred in 1917, today remains the world's record for all kinds of aircraft, airship or airplane.

Larger Zeppelins More Powerful

During the summer of 1918 the Zeppelins were again given higher climbing ability to meet the ever-increasing efficiency of planes and anti-aircraft guns. Another gas bag was added to the new ships

PLATE 23

Zeppelin-Werke Staaken Giant Biplane in Comparison With Pursuit Plane, 1916.
The Giant Biplane had a wing spread of 137.76 feet and carried a useful load of 4½ tons. Its power plant totaled 1250 horsepower and made a speed of 90 miles per hour.

Zeppelin-Dornier All Metal Pursuit Plane Type DO D1, 1918.
Note the absence of all struts and wire bracing.

(Plates 13 and 14), which brought them up to 2,189,220 cubic feet (62,000 cubic meters) capacity. In order not to diminish the speed two motors were added in respective gondolas, making seven engines in all, aggregating 1820 horsepower. They could carry 94,798 pounds (43,000 kilograms) or about 60% of their total lift. It was planned to add improvements enabling them to reach an altitude of 26,240 feet (8,000 meters) but the armistice halted all military activities and there was no occasion at that time for commercial craft to fly so high.

The Most Remarkable Scientific Development in the History of Aeronautics

Looking back over the development of the Zeppelins (Plate 15), one fails to find such remarkable and quick advance in any other medium of transportation. The history of engineering does not record in any other science progress comparable to that of the relatively new science of lighter-than-air as represented by the Zeppelins during the four years of war.

Seventy Percent Speed Increase

Their speed had increased from 46.6 to 87.5 miles per hour (75 to 130 kilometers per hour) approximately 70%. Their horsepower averaged 2,000. To carry useful loads of 44 tons their hydrogen capacity had been raised from 706,200 to 2,189,220 cubic feet (20,000 to 62,000 cubic meters). Other commercial ships were built embodying the improvements developed during the war. A description of them will be found in Chapter III.

Refinement in Design

This progress was made possible only by continuous experiments. Ideas and suggestions were adopted regardless of expense or chance of failure. In this way the Zeppelins had the advantage of every conceivable refinement in design. Their hulls, motor gondolas, in

PLATE 24

Zeppelin-Werke Staaken "Giant" All Metal Monoplane.

Which carried eighteen passengers in a luxurious cabin at a speed of 145 miles per hour. Power plant consists of 4-260 horsepower Maybach Motors totaling more than 1000 H. P.

Zeppelin-Dornier "Dragon Fly" All Metal Flying Boat, 1921.

Carries pilot and two passengers with 60 horsepower motor at a speed of 80 miles per hour and a gasoline consumption of only four gallons per hour.

fact, all braces and wires were streamlined so as to offer the least air resistance.

The rubberized cloth gas cells, or bags, used in 1914 had been discarded for others of light yet strong cotton cloth (and often silk), lined with goldbeater's skin to make them hydrogen proof.

Many of the experiments were as costly as they were painstaking but the Zeppelin engineers had learned early in their work that airships can not be built satisfactorily without long and arduous experiments to support each innovation. By continually striving to increase efficiency they secured simplified control systems and ships that handled more easily, hulls that were far more rigid yet lighter than their predecessors. Even the framework was lightened as by degrees it was made stronger. Many structural parts were standardized, facilitating production and repairs.

One has an idea of the innumerable parts necessary in the skeleton of a Zeppelin when he learns that more than 250,000 small crossties are required in making the triangular shaped girders in the frame work of a 1,977,300 cubic foot (56,000 cubic meters) ship which crosstie is a masterpiece of construction, because of its ingenious shape and finish.

Eighty-Eight Zeppelins During the War

Few persons know that during the war alone Luftschiffbau-Zeppelin designed and built 88 airships at their four great construction plants, as follows:

	1914	1915	1916	1917	1918	Total
At Friedrichshafen.........	6	19	14	14	8	59
At Potsdam..............	1	7	8	—	—	16
At Staaken...............	—	—	2	9	1	12
At Frankfort on Main.....	1	..	..	..	..	1
Total.................	8	26	24	23	9	88

(24)

PLATE 25

Zeppelin-Dornier "Dragon Fly" All Metal Flying Boat, 1921.
Wing span, 28 feet, weight empty 858 pounds. Water tight bulkheads are provided in side fins and wings.

Zeppelin-Dornier "Dragon Fly" All Metal Flying Boat, 1921.
With wings folded greatest width is only 10½ feet.

That in itself was a remarkable achievement which could have been accomplished only by possessing the scientific knowledge borne of experience. But it is not all.

One Hundred and Fifteen Zeppelins Built and Operated

From the day Count Zeppelin built his first ship until the last in 1919, a total of 115 Zeppelins were built and operated. The first three were experimental. Nine Zeppelins were successfully operated commercially in the transportation of passengers. Forty were delivered to the German army and 63 to the navy.

Scientific Comparison

There exists in the field of engineering an impartial, positive and unswerving means of determining the relative merits of things; and that is by a technical analysis of their success. By it one may recognize the values of the principles and construction methods involved. It is commonly said that nothing succeeds like success; and this is virtually true of the Zeppelins. Their record for efficiency remains unsurpassed, as a matter of fact, unequalled. It has never been denied that they were superior to contemporary craft or that they failed to maintain an increasing advantage over them.

This comparison is justified by the following figures which we will first attempt to explain.

It will be noted that there are three kinds of efficiency, (1) Speed (the aerodynamical figure), (2) Lift (the constructional figure) and (3) All-around efficiency (the combined quality figure).

The first relates to the efficiency of airship propulsion as effected by degrees of refinement in form, lessening of resistance, conservation of power, etc. It is simply the relation between the speed and engine power. Inasmuch as higher speed with the same power or the same speed with less power means economy of operation; therefore, the higher figure indicates superior quality.

PLATE 26

Zeppelin-Dornier "Dolphin" Monoplane All Metal Flying Boat Type DoCsII, 1920 Model.

Zeppelin-Dornier "Dolphin" Monoplane All Metal Flying Boat Type DoCsII, 1921 Model.
Carries six passengers besides pilot and mechanician. Speed 93 miles per hour, 185 horsepower
motor. Gasoline consumption 11.9 gallons per hour. Weight empty 3200 pounds.

Secondly, referring to the lift, this constructional figure indicates the relative useful or pay loads carried with the smallest amount of material used in the ship itself, because the ship, which must also be carried is "dead weight." As we must consider all ships equal as far as structural safety is concerned, the technical performance is determined by judging the relative performance in carrying useful loads (for ships of similar size), or equal loads with smaller ships, which means economy of operation. The higher figure indicates superior quality. It should be noted that this constructional figure is applicable only to comparison of airships of similar size, speed and service requirements. For general comparison, however, ships of approximately the same size may be considered.

Thirdly, all-around efficiency (the combined quality figure) is somewhat arbitrarily chosen by considering both the speed and carrying qualities together. It is not based on scientific deduction, but rather is a practical means of estimating general worth, as speed and carrying capacity are the main requirements of an airship.

PLATE 27

Zeppelin-Dornier "Komet" All Metal Monoplane, Type DoCIII, 1920 Model.

Zeppelin-Dornier "Komet" All Metal Monoplane.
Carries six passengers besides pilot and mechanician. One motor of 185 horsepower.

Efficiency Characteristics of Some of the Latest and Best Airships of All Nations

Nationality	Type and Name	Capacity Cubic Meters	Maximum Speed, Miles per Hour	Efficiency		
				Speed (1)	Lift (2)	All-round (3)
Non-Rigid Airships						
American.........	Goodyear Pony Blimp.......	990	40	24.2	0.60	15
French..........	Caussin T 2..............	9120	57.5	28.0	0.85	24
British..........	NS.....................	10200	57.2	25.6	0.65	17
German.........	PL27...................	31300	55.7	27.0	0.98	26
Italian..........	T 34 (Roma)............	34000	74.2	21.5	0.68	15
Rigid Airships						
British..........	R 80...................	34000	59.7	36.6	0.80	29
British..........	R 33—R 34.............	55500	59.7	37.3	0.75	28
British..........	R 36—R 37.............	59500	65.0	40.0	0.80	32
German.........	Schutte Lanz SL22........	56000	62.5	45.2	1.36	61
German.........	Zeppelin LZ 120 (Bodensee).	20000	82	63.7	0.76	48
German.........	Zeppelin LZ 121 (Nordstern).	22500	78.8	61.4	0.78	48
German.........	Zeppelin LZ 100..........	56000	67.2	56.0	1.59	89
German.........	Zeppelin LZ 113..........	62200	81	62.2	1.60	100
German.........	Zeppelin LZ 102..........	68500	63.7	54.4	1.90	103

Scientific deductions and formulae to be found in "Zeitschrift fur Flugtechnik und Motorluftschiffahrt," June 15th and June 30th, 1920, issues. Article by P. Jaray.

PLATE 28

Dr. Max freiher von Gemmingen.

Dr. Hugo Eckener

Kommerzienrat Alfred Colsman

Dr. Ing. Ludwig Dürr

Carl Maybach

CHAPTER II

The Zeppelin Organization at the Time of Its Greatest Activity
1918–1919

THE Zeppelin Endowment for the Propagation of Air Navigation (Zeppelinstiftung zur Foerderung der Luftfahrt) which Count Zeppelin founded with the subscription fund of 6,000,000 marks presented to him by the German people in 1908, is administered by a Board of Directors, of which Baron Max freiherr von Gemmingen, Zeppelin's nephew, who worked with him from the start, is Chairman. The other Directors are Baron von Bassus and Dr. Hugo Eckener.

The Zeppelin Endowment owns Luftschiffbau-Zeppelin (Zeppelin Airship Building Co.), the construction company organized in 1908 and controls the "DELAG" organized, as stated before, in 1910 for the operation of commercial Zeppelins. Interested in the "DELAG" are a number of financiers, though with all the others, it was under the personal supervision of Count Zeppelin, and after him the Directorate of the Zeppelin Endowment.

At the time of the Armistice the construction and operating companies employed 1,600 persons on their executive and engineering staffs and 12,000 workmen.

Many subsidiary companies were organized and operated, specializing in the various branches of Zeppelin work, experimenting and producing.

Many Subsidiary Companies

These subsidiary companies are also controlled by the Directorate. They were not permitted to disintegrate during the difficult period following the war, but instead, have kept their personnel and facilities

PLATE 29

Zeppelin Village (Zeppelindorf), 1916.
Constructed by the Zeppelin Airship Building Company for its employees and their families.

A Typical Double House.

A Typical Single House.

intact and are ready to continue the work which was interrupted by the terms of the treaty. They produce respectively motors, gas bags, propellers, gears, sheds and, in fact, everything pertaining to aerial navigation including airplanes, flying boats and parts.

The Construction Plants

The great construction plants are organized on the same principles as ship yards. Over them all is the General Director, Mr. Alfred Colsman, and Chief Engineer, Dr. Ing. Ludwig Duerr, the latter having been with Count Zeppelin since the first airship was started and to whom much of the credit must be given for the success attained.

There are various departments including the planning and supervising divisions, two designing divisions (one for scientific and general design, the other for workship and drawings), the manufacturing and erecting divisions, calculating and accounting, testing and controlling, and general maintenance divisions. The research department is a separate organization.

The Airship Factories

In the airship factories the framework is made and erected. The envelope is prepared, passenger and engine gondolas completed and assembled along with other apparatus and instruments. The power plant is built, excepting the motors and parts of the gear work. Research work along the lines of airship development is conducted there.

The original plant built at Friedrichshafen in 1910 included a double shed, workshops, offices and laboratory buildings. The shed would not accommodate ships of greater diameter than $52\frac{1}{2}$ feet (16 meters), so in 1914 new workshops and another shed was built, to be followed the next year by a still larger shed.

PLATE 30

The "DELAG" Passenger Zeppelin "Schwaben", 1912.

The "DELAG" Passenger Zeppelin "Schwaben", 1910.
Count Zeppelin and Doctor Eckener in the pilot car.

During 1915 and 1916 better workshops (Plate 16), offices and a larger laboratory, together with the largest wind tunnel on earth were completed, along with a low pressure chamber for testing motors, a new development as unique as it was important to the automotive science.

The Hydrogen Plant

The original hydrogen plant was enlarged to a capacity output of 353,100 cubic feet (10,000 cubic meters) daily, with storage facilities for 2,118,600 cubic feet (60,000 cubic meters). Since the war, the storage facilities have been reduced to 706,200 cubic feet (20,000 cubic meters) by order of the Allied Commission.

Powerful Radio Station

The Zeppelin wireless plant, started in 1910, has continued to develop with the science of radio and is now able to communicate with the United States.

The duralumin factory is capable of meeting all Zeppelin requirements.

The Great Zeppelin Hangars

The original shed, built in 1908-09 and first used in 1910, is now the ring building factory, where the great transverse frames for the Zeppelins are made. It is 603½ feet (184 meters) long, 150.8 feet (46 meters) wide and stands 65.6 feet (20 meters) high—huge dimensions in the early days but utterly dwarfed by the great sheds which have since appeared alongside. There are double doors at each end, one set operated on the turning, the other on the sliding principle. They are opened and closed by electricity in a few minutes.

In this shed twenty-eight Zeppelins were assembled, the last being LZ-39 after which it was devoted to the transverse ring frames.

PLATE 31

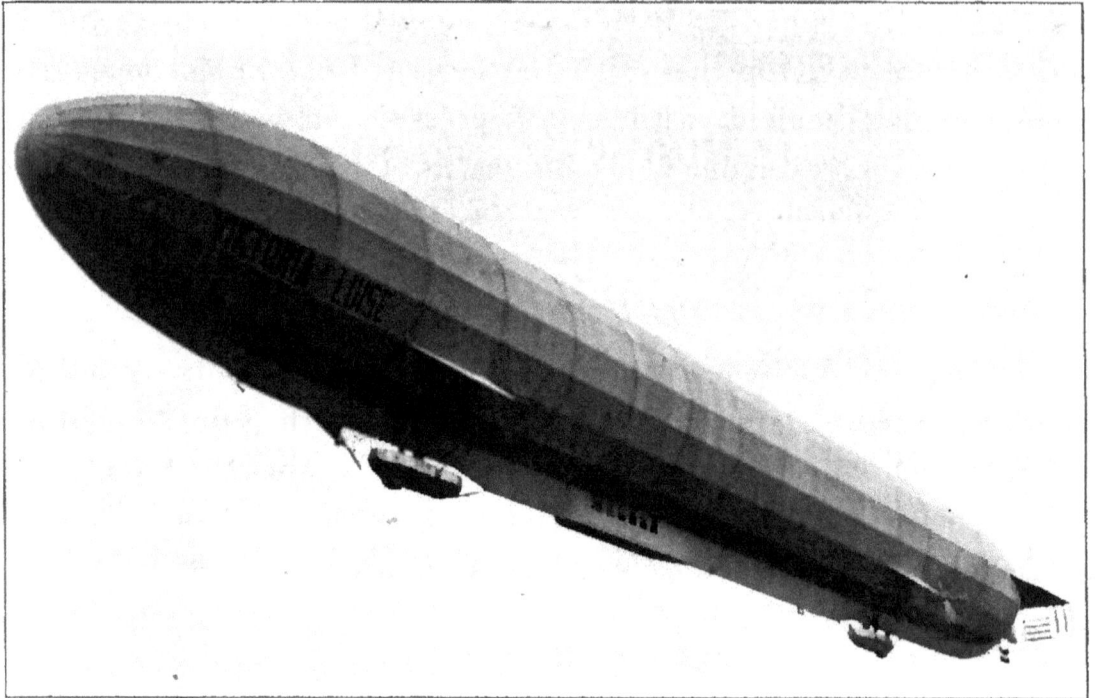

The "DELAG" Passenger Zeppelin "Victoria Louise", 1912.

The "DELAG" Passenger Zeppelin "Victoria Louise", 1912.

Twenty Zeppelins were built in the new shed, number one (Plate 16), which is 629.8 feet (192 meters) long, 129.23 feet (39.4 meters) wide and 91.8 feet (28 meters) high. Its double sliding doors are electrically operated.

Six of the larger Zeppelins were either built or reconstructed in another new shed, number two, erected to accommodate ships of 1,942,050 cubic feet (55,000 cubic meters) and more. It is 787.2 feet (240 meters) long, 150.8 feet (46 meters) wide and 114.8 feet (35 meters) high. Its sliding doors can be opened or closed within fifteen minutes. Both of the large sheds have long docking rails at each end which enables the Zeppelins to leave or return to shelter within a few minutes.

Another shed near the works at Loewental was turned over to Zeppelin by the Government. The Navy Zeppelin L-11 was built there in 1915. The last one was the navy ship L-72 which was completed as the armistice was signed. It was not inflated for delivery; and, therefore, remained the property of the Zeppelin Company.

In the spring of 1919 the L-72 was outfitted for a demonstration flight from Berlin to the United States and return; but it was prevented by the Allied Commissions which ordered it to be kept in the shed until delivered to France. All the Zeppelins assembled at Loewental were fabricated at the main plant and taken there only for final assembling of the parts.

The Potsdam Plant

The Zeppelin plant at Potsdam was erected in 1912 as an airship harbor and the following winter became one of the main construction centers with shed, workshops, and other necessary equipment. Here the passenger Zeppelin **"Sachsen"** was lengthened early in 1914. The last of the sixteen ships built there was the army

PLATE 32

The "DELAG" Passenger Zeppelin "Victoria Louise".
The ship's 1000th trip, totaling 40,000 miles in 1292 hours and during which 22,039 passengers
were carried without injury of any kind.

The "DELAG" Passenger Zeppelin "Victoria Louise".
Count Zeppelin and Doctor Eckener beneath the ship.

Zeppelin LZ-81 late in 1916, after which, because the shed was too small for the larger ships, it was used for building giant seaplanes. Later on it was converted into a special repair factory of all the airship motors. The airship personnel was transferred to the Staaken plant near Berlin.

The Colossal Staaken Plant

The Zeppelin-Staaken plant (Plate 17), located in the outskirts of Berlin is considered the most modern airship factory in the world.

Into it were put all the knowledge and experience of ten years of practical airship production. There were at one time two large sheds 820 feet (250 meters) long, 150.8 feet (46 meters) wide and 114.8 feet (35 meters) high, with a ring building shed between them, great workshops, research laboratories, administration building, hydrogen plant and all accessories.

The latest and most efficient machinery and tools then devised were provided. A large airdrome was constructed, as it was planned to make Staaken the postwar center of Zeppelin airship activity.

Here is was planned to locate both stationary and rotary sheds, the latter turning like a locomotive turn-table, making it possible to point their entrances in any direction the prevailing wind might dictate, to insure safe launching or landing of the Zeppelins. Then there were to be airplane factories on the same airdrome. It was at the Staaken plant that the L-59 was fabricated for the record flight to German East Africa and return. In all, twelve Zeppelins were built there.

The Duralumin Works

During the war two plants were put up in the vicinity of Friedrichshafen for making duralumin materials such as angle bars, strips, all kinds of girders, and other parts of the Zeppelin skeleton. They were operated for the most part with female labor.

PLATE 33

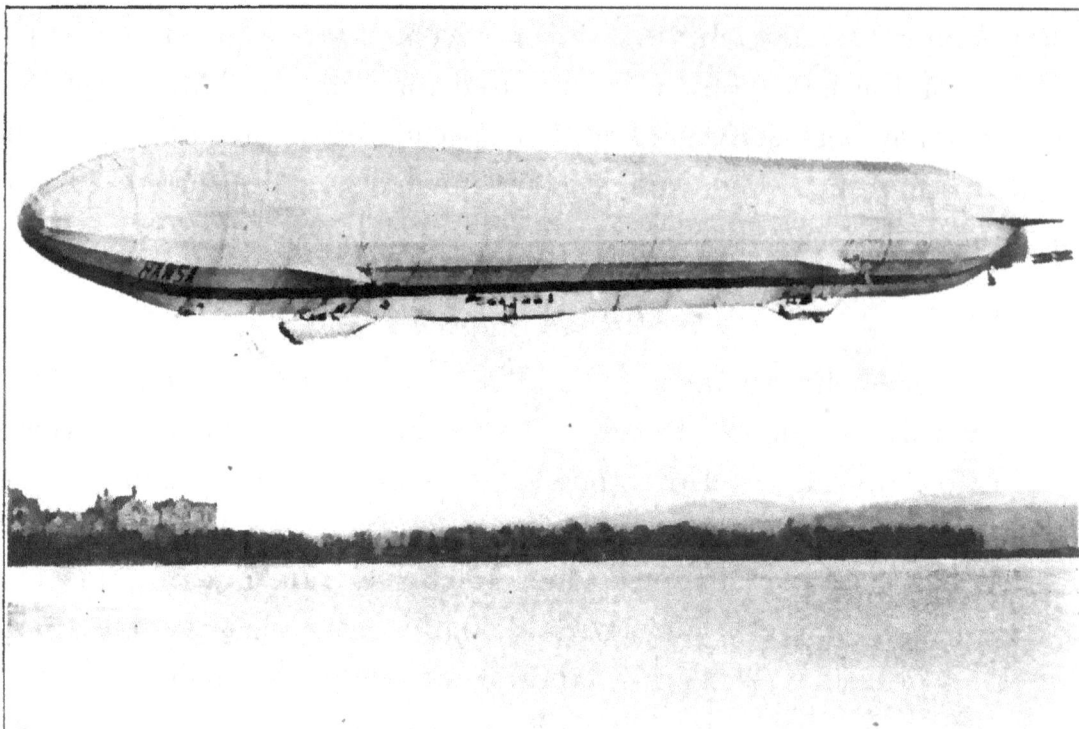

The "DELAG" Passenger Zeppelin "Hansa", 1912.

The "DELAG" Passenger Zeppelin "Sachsen", 1913.

The Woodworking Factory

A woodworking factory (Holzindustrie G.M.B.H.-Meckenbeuren) also was established near Friedrichshafen for the manufacture of propellers, etc. It has recently been enlarged and is operating at full capacity producing materials for buildings, dwellings, etc. During the war the specially designed Zeppelin propellers were made at Goeppingen.

The Maybach Motor Works

One of the accessory companies founded by Zeppelin in 1909 was the Maybach Motor Factory (Maybach-Motorenbau) (Plate 18), at Friedrichshafen. It was enlarged considerably during the war, supplying practically all the airship motors used. Today the Maybach works include three large three story factory buildings, parts of which are devoted to executive offices, two workshops of recent origin occupying two acres, many engine testing stands, laboratory, and a power plant fully equipped with the latest machinery. The entire plant is under the management of Mr. Maybach, inventor of the only motor designed for airships alone. One reason for the peculiar efficiency of the plant is the special workman's training department which has received considerable attention from the executives.

The first Maybach motors were produced in 1912 (Plate 19), and were 140 and 180 horsepower. They contributed largely to the success of the commercial Zeppelin before the war. In 1915 a 240 horsepower motor was built, and this was the principal motor used on the military and naval Zeppelins. Maybach produced an entirely new motor in 1917. It supplied from 260 to 320 horsepower and is noted as the first supercompression motor. Quickly recognized as the best engine for airplanes, it became the leading German aviation motor until late in 1918 when other motors built on similar prin-

PLATE 34

"DELAG"-Zeppelin Harbor at Frankfort a.M., 1912.

"DELAG"-Zeppelin Harbor at Baden-Baden, 1910.

ciples appeared and were found more adaptable to the planes. Maybach, meanwhile, developed other types (Plate 20), principally 160
and 260 horsepower units for heavier-than-air craft.

The following table illustrates the development in types and performance of engines:

Performance of Engines—1892-1918

Year	Motor	H. P.	Revolutions per Minute	Weight Kg.	Unit Weight Kg./H. P.	Fuel Consumption Gr./hp-hr
1892	Diamler............	11	440	500	45,5	500
1899	Diamler............	15	680	385	25,7	400
1905	Diamler............	90	1050	360	4,00	....
1907	Diamler............	100	1080	400	4,00	265–240
1909	Diamler............	115	1100	420	3,65	....
1910	Diamler............	120	1100	450	3,75	225
1910	Maybach............	145	1100	450	3,1	240
1913	Maybach............	180	1200	462	2,56	225
1914	Maybach............	210	1250	414	1,97	225
1915	Maybach............	240	1400	365	1,52	200
1917	Maybach............	260	1400	400	1,54	200
1918	Maybach............	260	1400	390	1,50	200

The Employment and Training System

Apprentices and girls are given a thorough examination and test
to determine their fitness for the work, which requires the utmost
accuracy. Then they enter a twelve weeks probationary service.
Their apprenticeship lasts four years. All apprentices are given
instruction by engineers and foremen in physics, chemistry, knowledge of materials, model making, foundry work, algebraic calcula-
tion methods, the handling of graphics, curves, statistics, price cal-
culation, machines and tools and particularly the principles and
functions of internal combustion engines.

On January 1st, 1918, 1980 workmen were employed, 416 of
them women. There were 57 women on the executive and office
staff of 217. On November 1st, that year, 3300 workmen and 349
others were employed, 599 of them women.

PLATE 35

"DELAG"-Zeppelin Harbor at Hamburg, 1912.

"DELAG"-Zeppelin Harbor at Leipzig, 1913.
"Sachsen" landing for first time after completion of harbor June 1913.

The Zeppelin-Maybach Gearless Car

In the fall of 1921 Maybach exhibited for the first time the 22–70 horsepower gearless motor car, designed to simplify operation. Only what is termed the direct speed is used in driving; except for grades of more than 10%, and for the starting on these grades, when apart from the rest of the mechanism a single gear is used by pushing down a pedal. When it is released, the direct grip is automatically restored without noise or vibration. Backing is accomplished with the electric starting motor by means of a pedal. Smaller cars of this type are now under construction.

New Methods of Gas Bag Fabrication

The early gas bags for the Zeppelins were made of rubberized cotton fabric. This material was comparatively heavy and further, it allowed the hydrogen gas to deteriorate during prolonged operations. Count Zeppelin experimented with various materials, particularly goldbeater skins, which are the big intestines of oxen and other cattle, treated until they become like leather and then they are very thin, tough and so durable that they wear much longer than fabric. Zeppelin learned that goldbeater's skins held gas better, also, and unlike rubberized fabric, practically eliminated the danger of electrical sparks due to friction or tearing.

He organized the Gasbag Manufacturing Company (Ballon-Hullen G.M.B.H.) at Templehof in 1912, to carry out this development and goldbeater's skins were used exclusively, as the loss of two Zeppelins that year was traced directly to the balloon fabric in the gas bags causing sparks which exploded the hydrogen. The ships were the LZ-12 and the Schwaben, the former exploding during inflation and the latter while moored at Dusseldorf.

The gold beater skins possess certain disadvantages, however. For one thing, they were difficult to handle because of their small

PLATE 36

"DELAG"-Zeppelin Harbors at Liegnitz and Dresden, 1913-14.

"DELAG"-Zeppelin Harbor and Manufacturing Plant at Potsdam (near Berlin), 1915.

size; so they were shingled on to thin cotton fabric. Since 1917 silk has been used, the combination when prepared being so light and thin as to be transparent. In fact, the Zeppelins hulls are themselves nearly transparent, the fabric envelope and gas bags being so thin that one can make out figures silhouetted on the opposite side of the hull when it faces the light.

The Tempelhof factory, with Mr. Trenkmann as Manager, now includes many buildings and workshops, several put up recently for dyeing and treating fabrics. During the war a thousand persons were employed. The gas bags used in all the German airships were made there; and the factory working with another firm under a patent license agreement, made a majority of the German observation balloons.

The Maag-Zeppelin Gear Works

It was not long after the war started that Count Zeppelin had difficulty in securing delivery of cog-wheels, etc. In 1915 he co-operated with Mr. Maag, a Swiss engineer, in starting the Friedrichshafen Cog-wheel and Gear Factory (Zahnradfabrik Friedrichshafen G.M.B.H), another subsidiary (Plate 18.) The plant is as modern as they could make it. The buildings occupy three acres. They include office buildings, workshops for hobbing, heat-treating, grinding and polishing cog-wheels and the complete gear transmissions. Aluminum castings are obtained from the foundry of the parent company, Luftschiffbau-Zeppelin.

The gear works is equipped throughout with automatic machines built on the Maag patents. His cog-wheel involves a new principle, giving utmost safety and freedom from wear and noise. Specially designed testing machines are used, guaranteeing precision of the gear wheels.

PLATE 37

"DELAG" Zeppelin Route Chart, 1912-13.

During the war the company made all the gearing on the Zeppelins and airplanes. The factory is now operating at full capacity, employing 500 men, making motor car gears, transmissions, etc. The manager is Dipl. Ing. Count von Soden.

The Hangar Construction Company

Back in 1913 a subsidiary was founded, first as a consulting engineering concern; but soon thereafter it became the Zeppelin Hangar Construction Company (Zeppelin Hallenbau G. M. B. H.). Through long practical experience it is prepared to build and equip complete airship harbors and dock yards, prepare landing fields and airdromes. One of the principal developments with which it has been accredited is the rotary shed, single or double. It has erected special workshops, gas plants and all the accessories of a modern flying terminal.

The company designed and constructed the two modern sheds at Friedrichshafen, the entire Staaken plant, the "DELAG" airship harbors and nearly all the other airports in Germany. Many hangars and workshops in Germany today were put up by the company using specially patented construction methods. In all some twenty-four complete airship harbors have been built from start to finish by this organization, which is under the management of Mr. Milatz and his staff of experts varying between 20 and a hundred members.

Zeppelin Production of Airplanes

In 1916, the airship building personnel conducted experiments with airplanes made of airship duralumin girders covered with fabric. The object was to secure a plane which would meet the technical requirements of aerial photography. Though their activities were devoted to the airship building programme, the engineers managed to produce an experimental machine of that type. On its

PLATE 38

"DELAG" Passenger Zeppelin "Bodensee".

first trials, it proved so superior to existing types that the army urgently requested early delivery of a number of machines. There was little time to do the work, however, and at the end of the war only twenty had been completed. They were destroyed, afterward, under the terms of the Versailles treaty.

There were other airplane enterprises organized by Count Zeppelin, which remain today leaders in their respective fields. Zeppelin was the first person to conceive of the giant all-metal flying boats (Plates 21 and 22), and all-metal airplanes.

The Zeppelin-Dornier Metal Monoplanes

He organized a small group within the parent company, Luffschiffbau-Zeppelin, in 1912. It was the first concern exclusively engaged in all-metal airplane construction. Today the great plant of Dornier Metallbau G. M. B. H. at Seemoos, near Friedrichshafen is noted the world over for its remarkable development in heavier-then-air craft, which are named Dornier, after the manager and chief engineer. From the first Count Zeppelin placed at the disposal of Claude Dornier ample funds with which he was able to follow utterly new and original methods in developing all-metal planes on a strictly scientific basis.

It had never been done before. The plant in six years developed from a small experimental workshop to one of the largest in the world. At Seemoos there are located a great hangar, office buildings, workshops, turntables, slips and other facilities for landing and withdrawing the huge Dornier flying boats. Another great factory was erected at Lindau in 1918 but has not been used for reasons of economy.

As progress was made in designing, constructing and testing metal planes, Dornier devoted the work practically toward perfection of internally braced monoplanes. The monoplane principle

PLATE 39

The "DELAG" Passenger Zeppelin "Nordstern", 1919.
A sister ship of the "Bodensee."

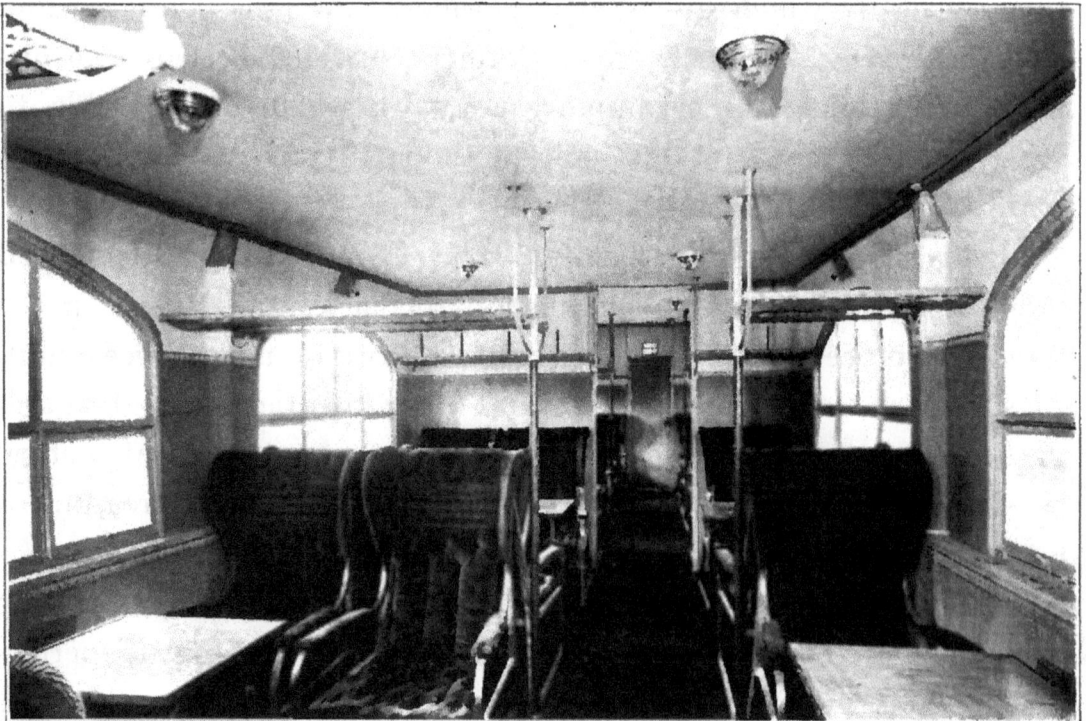

The "DELAG" Passenger Zeppelin "Nordstern."
Interior view of the passenger cabin.

was maintained from the beginning. Today it is recognized generally as the most desirable type. New designs, methods of handling metal, experiments with various kinds of construction, newly invented machine tools, experimental planes and models, each an advance in efficiency, invariably something newly discovered in the infant science of aerodynamics—these were the activities of Dornier and his staff in six years.

The results were Dornier's all-metal planes, possessing from 55 to 2,400 horsepower. They had just started quantity production of big planes and flying boats in the factories at Lindau and Seemos when the German revolution halted all activities. Since then, though hampered by the treaty stipulations, the company has developed a series of commercial types unexcelled in construction, performance and safe operation. Since the war both commercial land planes and flying boats powered with from one to three engines have been produced.

Twenty-one Dornier Designs

During the war their products included pursuit planes, single motor two-place fighters (Plate 23), two and three motored bombing planes and four and multi-engined giant planes—all for over land flying. Seaplane types included single engine two-place fighters, two and three motored flying boats and four and multi-engine giant flying boats. More than one hundred domestic patents were held and more than 250 filed in foreign patent offices. Twenty-one different designs for experimental types had been produced, seventeen of them worked out in as many machines which were flown, and four Plates 24-25-26-27 made into models Plates 24-25-26-27. The following is a list of the experimental personnel year by year:

	1915	1916	1917	1918	1919	1920
Engineers.......	15	25	25	69	52	23
Workmen.......	30	250	300	547	207	80

PLATE 40

The "DELAG" Passenger Zeppelin "Bodensee."
Landing at Friedrichshafen September 1919.

The "DELAG" Passenger Zeppelin "Bodensee."
Floating in the large shed at Friedrichshafen.

Zeppelin Builds Giant Airplanes

But there was another angle to the Zeppelin airplane activities. Count Zeppelin held the rank of General in the German Army. He had long been in a position which kept him informed of the needs of the fighting forces. For several months after the declaration of war he observed the heavy tasks to which his airships were put and then undertook the development of larger airplanes, far larger than any existing in the world at the time.

He consulted the noted aviator Hillmuth Hieth, and together they conferred with Professor Baumann of the technical university at Stuttgart. Bauman was already noted for his work as an aeronautical engineer. Within a few months they produced a multi-engined giant bomber. It proved successful. To produce these machines in quantity the Zeppelin works at Staaken were erected at the same time as the airship building plant. The airplane factory at Staaken soon employed more than a thousand men in turning out the giant night bombers, numbers of which were flown in the raids over London and Paris in 1917 and 1918.

The Airplane Works at Staaken

The plant at Staaken was complete, including two great airplane assembling sheds, workshops, offices, etc. It is now closed. Other German firms have built similar bombing planes under the Zeppelin patents. Twenty-six of them were built at Staaken, however.

They had a 137.76 foot (42 meters) wing span, carried 4.5 tons useful load, could climb to a height of 14,760 feet (4,500 meters) with their motors which aggregated 1,250 horsepower. Their average speed was 90 miles per hour (Plate 23).

Other machines were built, smaller, but of all-metal construction. After the war "The Staaken Giant" (Plate 24) was put into commission. It, too, was all-metal, carried four motors and was

PLATE 41

The "DELAG" Passenger Zeppelin "Nordstern."
Leaving Friedrichshafen for France. Note the progressive increase in the size of the sheds.

The "DELAG" Passenger Zeppelin "Bodensee."
Passengers enjoying an excursion over Berlin.

distinctly a commercial plane. During many successful trials it carried eighteen passengers at a speed of 145 miles an hour. Later on, a two-engine commercial land plane was nearing completion when the Inter-allied Aeronautical Commission ordered all work stopped, and the activities at Staaken ceased.

Social Welfare Institutions of the Zeppelin Organizations

One of the main requisites for success in any industry is the welfare of the men and women employed; and the establishment of the great Zeppelin organization created a community of employes in the small town on Lake Constance which demanded increasing attention as the organization expanded.

At first questions of industrial and social welfare were settled by a special department within Liffschiffbau-Zeppelin, but in September, 1913, a separate organization (Zeppelin Wohlfabrit G. M. B. H.) was provided. Count Zeppelin specified that homes for the men be provided immediately; that they should be built "economically but that they should make for comfort." One hundred and one single family houses were completed in July, 1916, and the new community was named Zeppelindorf (Zeppelin village) (Plate 29). Each house sits in a garden which enables the occupant to raise his own vegetables and fruits.

The club house was opened in March, 1917. Here is a large dining room for the workmen, which is also used for concerts, plays, meetings and other social activities. There are several club rooms. Nearby are the laundry, ice plant, steam plant, and other common utilities. The "Inn" and general store are also patronized by the people of Friedrichshafen.

Later an agricultural department was established for the purpose of supplying good food at low prices. Five large farms are worked by this branch and cattle raising and fruit growing have made it one of the most notable institutions in Central Europe.

PLATE 42

The "DELAG" Passenger Zeppelin "Bodensee."
The crew at the finish of the ship's 100th flight between Berlin and Friedrichshafen, December 1919.

The "DELAG" Passenger Zeppelin "Nordstern."
Control car, front view.

There is a savings bank which pays slightly more than the ordinary interest rate which followed the erection of the public library where all employees are encouraged in self-instruction. All sorts of scientific books, popular works and magazines are provided, beside the many lectures. Courses in domestic science are held for the women.

There was so much building to be done that a brick factory became one of the most important institutions in Zeppelin Village, which has also acquired an athletic field under the direction of an instructor in physical culture.

Practically the same community, with all the institutions, etc., has been created for the Zeppelin workers at Staaken, on the outskirts of Berlin.

PLATE 43

The "DELAG" Passenger Zeppelin "Nordstern."
Elevator Rudder and Altitude Controls.

Chief Engineer's Station Engine Telegraphs.

Steering Wheel and Compass.

CHAPTER III

Operations of Commercial Zeppelins

TTRACTED by Count Zeppelin's earlier flights, hundreds of persons made reservations for the regularly conducted commercial trips, when in 1910 he organized the Deutsche Luftschiffart, A. G. (German Air Ship Transportation Co.), briefly called the "DELAG" There was apparently a popular demand for commercial airship transport. Zeppelin founded the "DELAG" to meet this demand, and also to provide operating personnel and train pilots and crews for the other services, which he knew, would be necessary in case of emergency.

The "DELAG" was capitalized for 3,000,000 marks (approximately $714,000) and while it was a subsidiary of Luftschiffbau-Zeppelin, there also participated in this commercial operating organization a number of capitalists, whose faith in commercial air transport was fully justified by the success of the "DELAG" despite much difficulty the first year or so due to lack of meteorological data and inexperience.

The First Air Transport Company

During the latter part of 1910, minor accidents occurred which sometimes damaged the airships and disrupted the service, but in 1911 a comparatively regular service was established and maintained. The principal ship was the **"Schwaben,"** (Plates 5 and 30) which was far superior to her predecessors and which had the advantage of new and larger sheds at the Zeppelin-"DELAG" airports. The schedule maintained by the **"Schwaben"** justifies the assertion that the "DELAG" operated the first commercial aerial transport company on earth. Her success encouraged expansion, and in 1912, two

PLATE 44

The "DELAG" Passenger Zeppelin "Bodensee."
On an excursion over lake district near Potsdam.

The "DELAG" Passenger Zeppelin "Bodensee."
Passengers at Friedrichshafen embarking for Berlin.

additional ships, the **"Victoria Louise"** (Plates 31-32) and the **"Hansa"** (Plate 33) were built and entered the "DELAG" service, to be followed the next year by the **"Sachsen"**, (Plate 33).

Part of the Aviation Reserve

The German Army commandeered all these commercial Zeppelins at the start of the war. They were used partly for military duty and partly as training ships for the many necessary crews. The first year of the war, they added hundreds of flights to the commercial record they had already made; but gradually became obsolete and were dismantled to make room for the newer and more efficient types being turned out at the Zeppelin Plants.

The headquarters of the "DELAG" were at Frankfort. It was from that city that the chief executives controlled operations. The Business Manager had charge of the financial and commercial activities. He supervised salaries, purchase of supplies, materials, etc. Flying operations were in charge of a Director of Flight. He had charge of the personnel at the air harbors; and all technical problems were put up to him.

The crew of a commercial Zeppelin included the pilot, a reserve pilot, a flight mechanic, helmsmen and engineers, the number depending on the nature of the flight, a wireless operator and a ship's steward. The crew usually aggregated twelve men.

Created the First Airship Harbor

As far as practicable, each Zeppelin was assigned to a definite air harbor, which was known as its home station, or terminal. Here all the repairs and maintenance were done. The members of the crew were assigned to suitable homes, all located in that immediate vicinity. The maintenance crews for airships and sheds were also stationed there. These auxiliaries averaged thirty persons under the

PLATE 45

The "DELAG" Passenger Zeppelin "Bodensee."
Crew's Quarters.

Water Ballast Bag, Capacity 300 Kilos.

Wireless Room.

direction of a foreman. They, too, formed the nucleus for the landing party necessary to handle the airships on arrival or departure. Each air harbor had a manager and his assistants to handle business details.

When the Zeppelin arrived at its home port, and during its sojourn there the pilot was in sole command of both ship and air station. He was held strictly accountable for the safety of his ship; and acted as both station master and flying officer, subject only to instruction from the Director of Flight. The pilot alone made the decisions as to whether or not he should make a flight, when he should start and the number of passengers and crew he would carry. It is interesting to note that this system was adopted for the entire German airship force during the war. In fact, practically all airship personnel was trained by the "DELAG."

Like Land and Water Services

There was no special organization for selling passenger accommodations. Agents of the Hamburg-American Line ("HAPAG") which had offices in all German cities, also represented Zeppelin, and reservations were made on the same basis as for ocean going vessels.

The **"Deutschland"** was the first Zeppelin operated by the "DELAG." The motors, however, were not very dependable; and the low speed of the ship, combined with lack of experience made it susceptible to minor accidents. The **Deutschland** was so badly damaged, finally, that Zeppelin was compelled to rebuild her. During the period that she was being reconstructed the Zeppelin LZ-6 was substituted.

The "Schwaben" Filled all Requirements

The first ship to fill the requirements essential to safe and steady commercial operations was the **"Schwaben"** built in the summer of 1911. She was 459.2 feet (140 meters) long, 45.9 feet (14 meters) in

PLATE 46

The "DELAG" Passenger Zeppelin "Nordstern."
Interior view with gas bags removed.

diameter, and of 615,580 cubic feet (18,000 cubic meters) hydrogen gas capacity. Her three Maybach 145 horespower motors gave the "**Schwaben**" a speed of 43 miles an hour (19.3 meters per second). She had a useful lift of 8,818.4 pounds (4,000 kilograms). During the latter part of 1911 more than a hundred flights were made with the "**Schwaben**" between Lake Constance, Niederheim, Gotha, and Berlin. These flights warranted larger ships.

In March 1912, the "DELAG" put into operation the new Zeppelin "**Victoria Louise**" (Plates 31-32) and in the summer, her sister ship the "**Hansa**". These Zeppelins were 485.4 feet (148 meters) long and 45.9 feet (14 meters) in diameter. They each held 670,890 cubic feet (19,000 cubic meters) of hydrogen and their useful lift was 11,023 pounds (5,000 kilograms). Motors had been so improved that the "**Victoria Louise**" and "**Hansa**" were able to make 44.7 and 46.9 miles per hour respectively.

Accommodations for Many Passengers

Each Zeppelin accommodated twenty-four passengers besides the crew. Warm meals were served from the up to date electrical kitchen. There was wireless aboard, also.

The ships gave complete satisfaction during hundreds of flights made over constantly increasing distances. They won the confidence of the traveling public; and equally important, had supplied much valuable experience and information, for they operated in all kinds of weather at all seasons of the year.

In 1913, the new Zeppelin, "**Sachsen**", (Plate 33) was added to the "DELAG" fleet. She had a length of 459.2 feet (140 meters) and a diameter of 49.2 feet (15 meters) which increased the lift because she carried 670,890 cubic feet (19,000 cubic meters) of hydrogen which gave her a useful lift of more than 13,227.6 pounds (6,000 kilograms). Her speed was better than 48 miles an hour and she carried twenty-four passengers.

PLATE 47

The "DELAG" Passenger Zeppelin "Bodensee."
Interior view gas bags not inflated.

New and larger sheds were built for the "DELAG" as the fleet increased in size. When they first commenced flying there were only two airship sheds in addition to the one at Friedrichshafen. These were at Baden-Baden and at Dusseldorf. They owned the shed at Baden-Baden and leased from the municipality the one at Dusseldorf. Toward the end of 1911 others were available, one at Johannisthal near Berlin and one at Gotha. In 1912 two more were ready, one at Frankfort on the main, owned by the "DELAG," and one at Potsdam, owned by Luftschiffbau-Zeppelin. In 1913 the municipalities of Hamburg, Leipzig and Dresden erected sheds. (Plates 34-35-36.) In the beginning the sheds were single but the ones built after the "DELAG" had started regular schedules, accommodated two ships side by side. Some of the sheds were huge, often 196.8 feet (60 meters) wide.

Development of Adequate Hangars

They were provided with electric lights, water supply and docking rails, which extended from either end. Special piping conveyed the hydrogen from plant to shed. All sheds had railway connections, and were equipped with waiting rooms for passengers and crews, as well as workshops and accessory buildings. The airship harbors built by the "DELAG" and Zeppelin had particularly extensive workshops, for besides the regular maintenance work, they produced many new parts and instruments for navigating Zeppelins.

At every shed there was a meteorological station fitted with barometers, barographs, thermographs, and a theodolite for measurement of the wind velocity in the upper atmosphere. Weather observations were made each morning and telegraphed to all other stations. This enabled all Zeppelin pilots to be thoroughly informed before setting out on a flight. The special data supplied by the Zeppelin stations was more adequate for airship requirements than

PLATE 48

The "DELAG" Passenger Zeppelin "Bodensee."
Power gondola (side) containing one 260 horsepower Maybach motor. Note ladder communicating with interior of ship.

The "DELAG" Passenger Zeppelin "Bodensee."
Power gondola (rear) containing two 260 horsepower Maybach motors. Note ladder communicating with interior of ship.

that from the Government official weather bureau. Wireless equipment was installed late in 1913.

Many Long Commercial Flights

The average commercial flight was from 37 to 62 miles (60 to 100 kilometers) from 1½ to 2½ hours. When the flights were from one airship harbor to another they often lasted four and sometimes eight hours. The fare was determined by the length of the flight, or the mileage. Round trip flights, which were comparatively short, cost from 25 to 50 dollars (one to two hundred marks.) The long distance trips ranged from 60 to 150 dollars (250 to 600 marks). Many single flights were made over the North Sea. The **"Victoria Louise"** often flew to Helgoland, Sylt and Norderney, the **"Hansa"** to Copenhagen and the **"Sachsen"** to Vienna. These flights were characterized as pleasure trips; and as such none was undertaken during the winter months. Instead, the Zeppelins underwent a thorough overhauling. Sometimes, however, a Zeppelin was kept in service all winter to train airship personnel of the army or navy.

Naturally "DELAG" became noted for its successful operations; and its ships were repeatedly chartered by the military or naval personnel for training flights.

Developed Airship Navigation

The "DELAG" has been credited with the entire development of airship navigating technique. For one thing, it was the only organization of its kind, training airship personnel in practical operations. The "DELAG" airships and airship crews were used almost exclusively for training purposes when war was declared. At that time there were two other airship construction companies in Germany, Schutte-Lanz and Parseval. Both of these organizations procured their airship pilots from the trained personnel of the "DELAG."

PLATE 49

The "DELAG" Passenger Zeppelin "Nordstern."
Rear view of rear power gondola containing two 260 horsepower Maybach motors.

Zeppelins Operated Safely

All of the flights listed in the following table were made without a single injury to passengers or crew. The **Deutschland** had been repeatedly damaged while entering or leaving her shed and was rebuilt. The **"Schwaben"** was burned at her moorings during a severe storm. It is now known that all these accidents could have been avoided, in view of the progress that has been made in the science of lighter-than-air. Experience has materially increased the performance and qualities of safety in airships. Better motors, controls, gas bags and other parts of the Zeppelin have been so improved as to preclude possibility of accidents such as those which occasionally hindered the operations of "DELAG" before the war. Each of the flights listed here averaged two hours, 68 miles (109 kilometers), traversed with 22 passengers. All the flights aggregated 107,180 miles (172,535 kilometers), more than *four times the girth of the earth at the equator.*

Commercial Operations of the Zeppelin

Airships	Number of Flights	Hours	Total Mileage in Kilometers	Number of Passengers Carried
"Deutschland" and the LZ-6........	62	124	6546	1778
"Schwaben".....................	218	480	27321	4354
"Victoria Louise"...............	489	981	54312	9738
"Hansa"........................	399	841	44437	8521
"Sachsen"......................	419	741	39919	9837
Total.......................	1588	3167	172535	34228

PLATE 50

The "DELAG" Passenger Zeppelin "Bodensee."
Front and rear views of rear power gondola. Note radiator temperature control and ladder.

The "DELAG" Passenger Zeppelin "Bodensee."
Interior view showing location of fuel tanks.

Trained Germany's Airship Forces

In the early days of the war the **"Victoria Louise"** made more than a thousand training flights for more than 39,852 miles (64,152 kilometers) in 1292 hours, flying time, all after she had been added to the military training forces. Finally, her framework became so worn that she was dismantled. The **"Sachsen"** and **"Hansa"** (Plate 33) performed similar service.

From the Managing Director to the mechanics, all of the "DELAG" personnel entered the service during the war, where they were instructors, and it was due to them that the numbers of Zeppelins launched for war service were manned by crews qualified to operate them.

Commercial Operations Resumed

The real work for which the "DELAG" was created, "to develop commercial air transport" was of necessity put aside during the period of the war, but these activities were resumed early in 1919 when it was decided to start a regular daily passenger service, at first between Berlin and Friedrichshafen, a distance of 373 miles (600 kilometers) and afteward extend it to Switzerland, Italy, Spain in the south and to Sweden in the north. The pre-war personnel of the "DELAG" was assembled at Friedrichshafen and the route to Berlin started by the new Zeppelin **"Bodensee"** on August 24th, 1919 (Plate 38).

The "Bodensee" an Improved Type

The **"Bodensee"** was designed and built in six months (January to July 1919), by Lufschiffbau-Zeppelin. She was the same size as the pre-war Commercial Zeppelins, *but had twice the engine power, carried twice their useful load and maintained a speed equal with the former ships using only one-half of their engine power.*

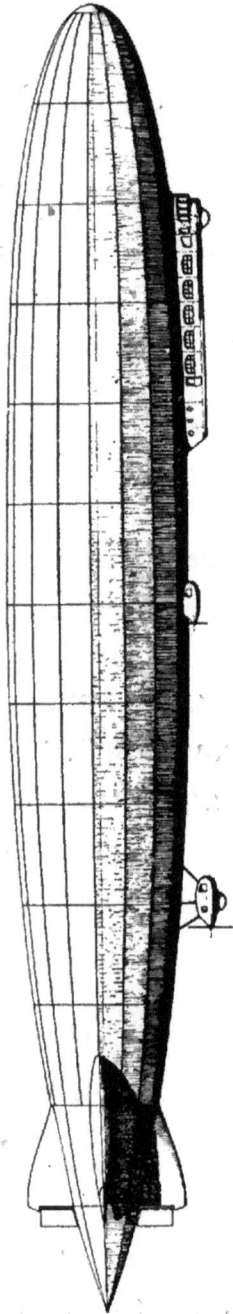

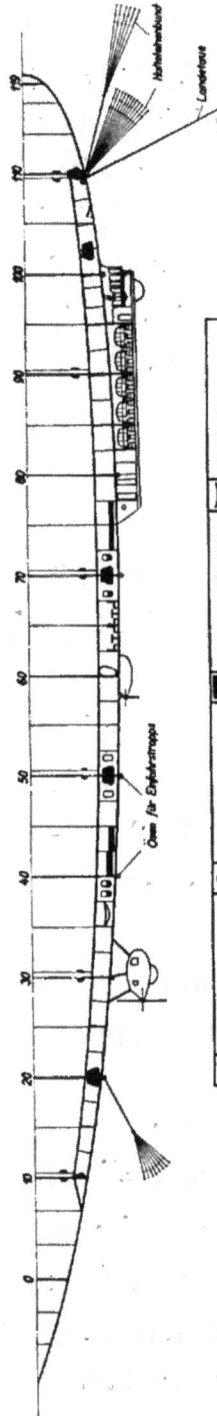

PLATE 51

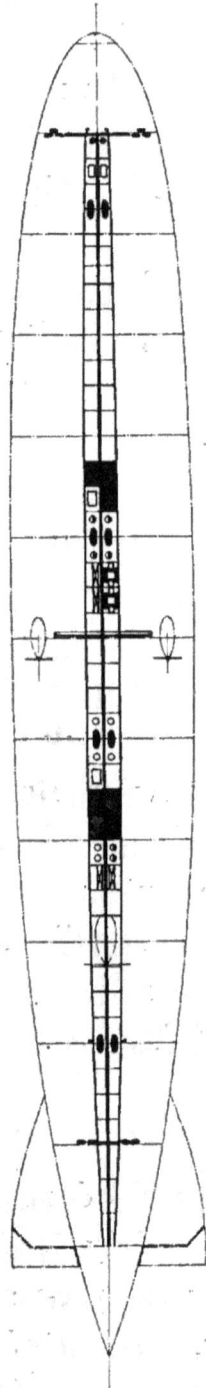

20–30,000 Cubic Meter Fast Passenger Zeppelin "Bodensee" Type.

The **"Bodensee"** was 426.4 feet (130 meters) long, after she had been lengthened by 32.8 feet (10 meters). Her diameter was 61.3 feet (18.7 meters) and she carried 794,475 cubic feet (22,500 cubic meters) of hydrogen. Her useful load normally was 25,353 pounds (11,500 kilograms). Her four motors were of 260 horsepower each. They turned three direct-driven propellers, one in each of the port and starboard motor gondolas which hung from the sides of the ship. The third propeller was driven by two engines in the rear motor gondola. The propellers averaged from 1,300 to 1,400 revolutions a minute. The **"Bodensee"** was capable of making 80 miles an hour. Her cruising speed was 75 miles an hour.

Carried Thirty Passengers

At this pace she could carry thirty passengers comfortably. They were seated in a luxurious salon (Plate 41) built in the pilot car under the forward part of the Zeppelin. Nearby in the same car were a kitchen and lavatory.

The **"Bodensee"** was maintained on the Friedrichshafen-Berlin route to experiment further in commercial air transport. While the "DELAG" did not attempt to make a profit, expenses were kept as low as possible and the prospects of monetary returns were generally favorable.

One Hundred and Three Flights in Ninety-Eight Days

From August 24th until December 1st, 1919, the **"Bodensee"** made 103 flights in 98 days; on several days making two flights, one a short sightseeing trip over Berlin in addition to her regular run. Seventy-eight flights were made between Lake Constance and Berlin and two between Berlin and Stockholm, eighty trips on schedule in ninety-eight days. There was no flying for ten days owing to general overhaul and repairs. On three occasions the regular flights were

PLATE 52

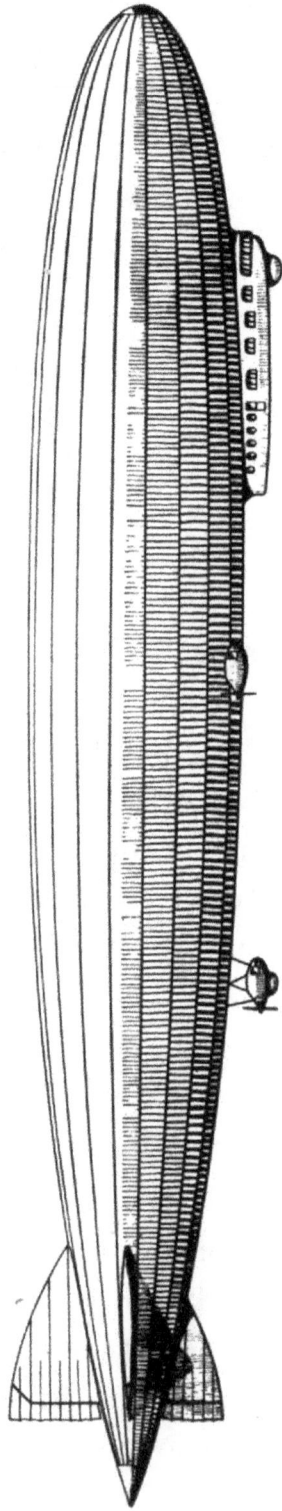

50,000 Cubic Meter Passenger Zeppelin.
For medium distances and training purposes.

postponed because of heavy cross winds which made it difficult and dangerous to start the Zeppelin from the fixed shed of the airdrome at Staaken. This meant the loss of six trips. Two of the regular trips were omitted because of the flights to Sweden.

Nevertheless, in that period 2,380 passengers were carried, exclusive of crews, about 11,000 pounds (5,000 kilograms) of mail and 6,600 (300 kilograms) of express, freight and baggage. The "Bodensee" was in the air 533 hours, flying in all 32,300 miles (52,000 kilometers) an average of 62 miles an hour. Notwithstanding the many unforeseen difficulties due to uncertain political and economic conditions in Germany during the last quarter of 1919, the technical results of the "Bodensee" operations were excellent.

The "Nordstern" a Sister Ship

A sister ship of the "Bodensee" was built during the last quarter of 1919, and named the "Nordstern" but in December, that year, the Inter-Allied Air-Control Commission ordered the airship operations stopped. The "Bodensee" was delivered to Italy and the "Nordstern" to France in 1921.

Once more the aeronautical world became interested in Zeppelins. The last cruise of the "Bodensee" under German management took her from Friedrichshafen to Rome. She cruised over Zurich, Bern, Geneva and Avignon, often making 160 kilometers an hour, to the Mediterranean, near St. Rafael. Visitors at Cannes, Nice and Monaco saw a rigid airship for the first time as the "Bodensee" held to her route passing directly over Corsica and Elba, and finally to the airdrome in Ciampino, between Rome and the Albanian mountains. She had made more than 825 miles (1,329 kilometers) in 12 hours and 49 minutes, at an average speed of 64.6 miles (104 kilometers) an hour for the entire distance.

PLATE 53

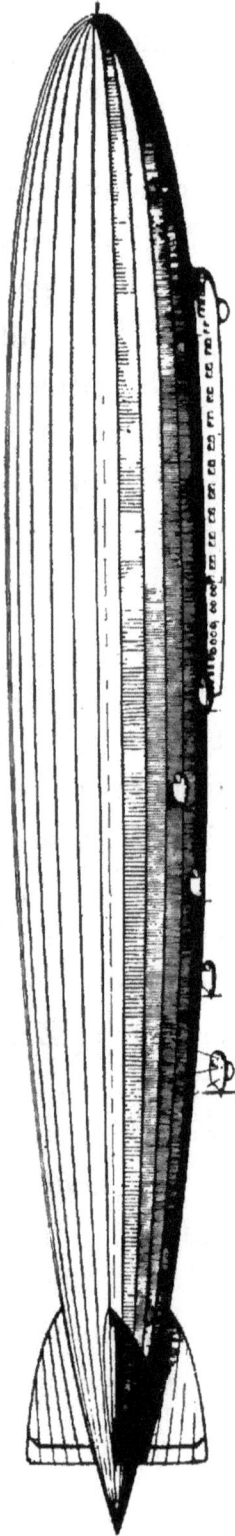

60,000 Cubic Meter Fast Passenger Zeppelin.

For medium distances. Accomodations for eighty passengers besides the necessary crew.

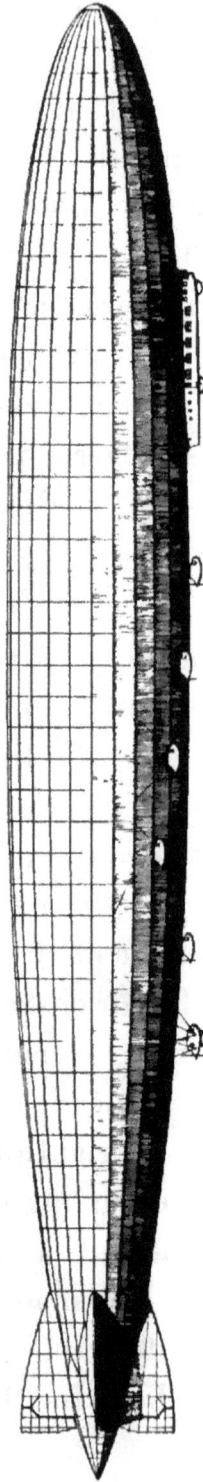

100,000 Cubic Meter Fast Commercial Zeppelin.

Trans-Atlantic mail and express service.

CHAPTER IV

The Zeppelin Organization and Facilities Today

THE Zeppelin organization today is prepared to build, deliver and operate rigid airships for any purpose. It has under contract virtually all the competent airship personnel in Germany. Practically all the engineering staffs and workmen employed in developing Zeppelins have been retained, one way or another, that they may be prepared to guarantee satisfactory performance of any Zeppelin turned out.

Actual construction work was discontinued early in 1920. The Allied Powers so interpreted the Treaty of Versailles that the German aircraft industry was not able to produce ships or planes having the least possible military value. Further restrictions were defined in the London Ultimatum. They have been enforced by the Allied Control Commission.

Research and Development Work Continues

Notwithstanding this severe handicap, the Zeppelin organizations have been kept intact. There has been sufficient work on motor cars, motor boats, motors, gears, aluminum foundry work, etc. to keep the workmen occupied. Where some of the plants have been closed, the entire personnel has been transferred into the other active organizations. In each branch of the Zeppelin organization design and research work on airships and aerial navigation have continued and progressed.

Zeppelin Able to Produce All Types

Luftschiffbau-Zeppelin has been particularly active in developing as far as possible the many ideas and inventions originating before and during the war. Many of their new airship designs have

PLATE 54

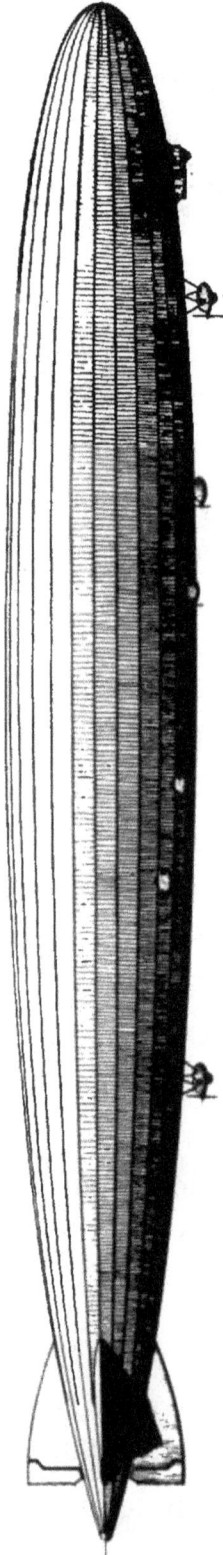

100,000 Cubic Meter Fast Commercial Zeppelin.
Trans-Atlantic mail and express service.

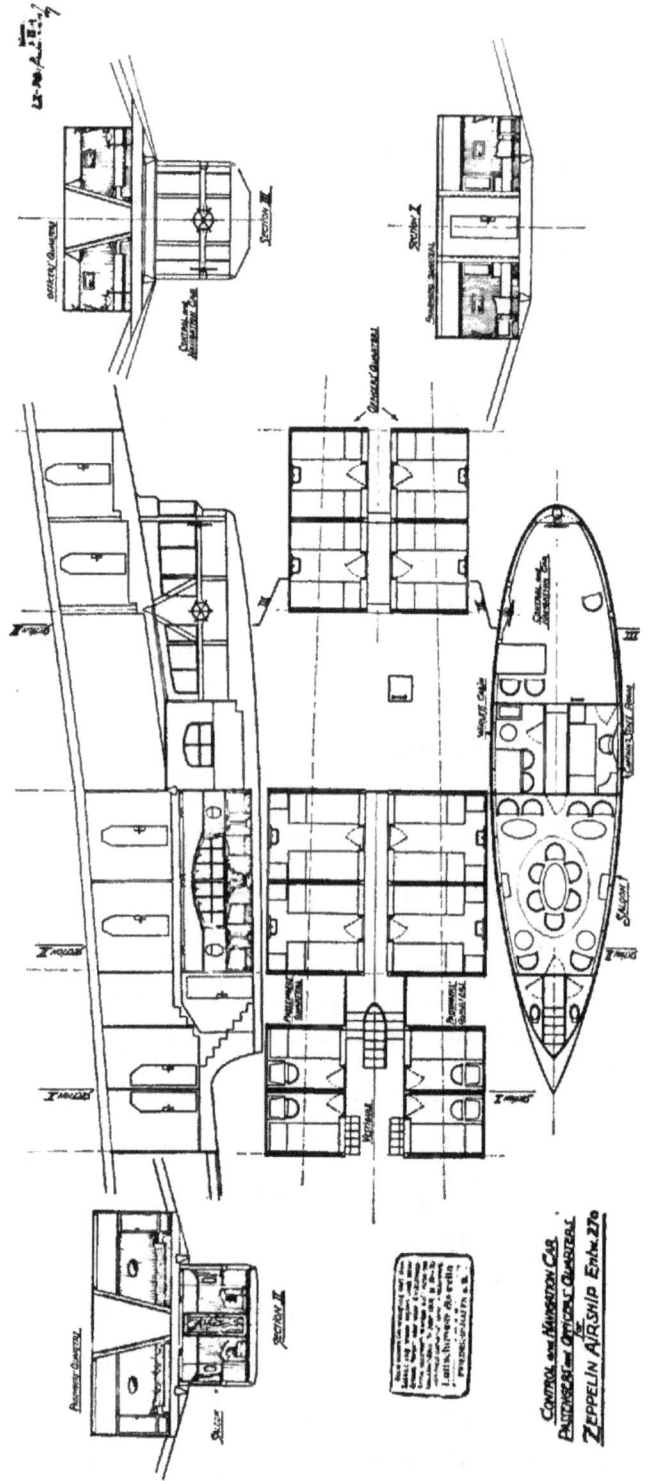

been completed, others partly finished. It is now possible to produce quickly any type of commercial airship from of 700,000 to 7,000,000 cubic feet (20,000 to 2,000,000 cubic meters) capacity.

Some of the principal types for which specifications have been completed and the performance of which are guaranteed and further, backed by more than twenty-five years of experience, include:

Plate 51   1—A 20,000 to 30,000 cubic meter fast passenger Zepelin, based on the **Bodensee** performance.

Plate 52   2—A 50,000 cubic meter passenger Zeppelin for medium distances and training purposes.

Plate 53   3—A 60,000 cubic meter fast passenger Zeppelin for medium distances.

Plate 53-54 4—A 100,000 cubic meter trans-atlantic mail-carrying Zeppelin.

Plate 55   5—A 135,000 cubic meter long distance passenger Zeppelin.

Airships for national defense are available, such as scouting, long distance patrol ships and others for mine spotting and short radius patrol.

Guaranteed Performance Based on Actual Experience

From actual experience during the war Luffschiffbau-Zeppelin is able to build and guarantee the performance of airplane carrying airships which permit large or small planes being launched or taken aboard while in flight.

Bombing and raiding airships have been developed; but on the other hand the military development is considered of secondary importance to the vast amount of knowledge and experience acquired for commercial airship operations.

PLATE 55

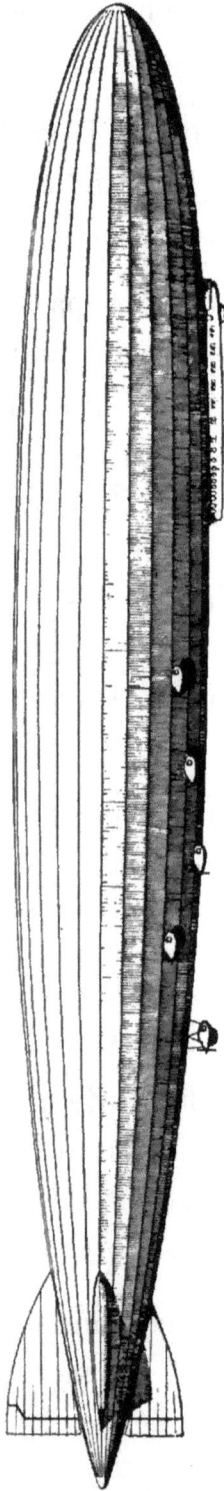

135,000 Cubic Meter Fast Passenger Zeppelin.
For long distance passenger and mail service.

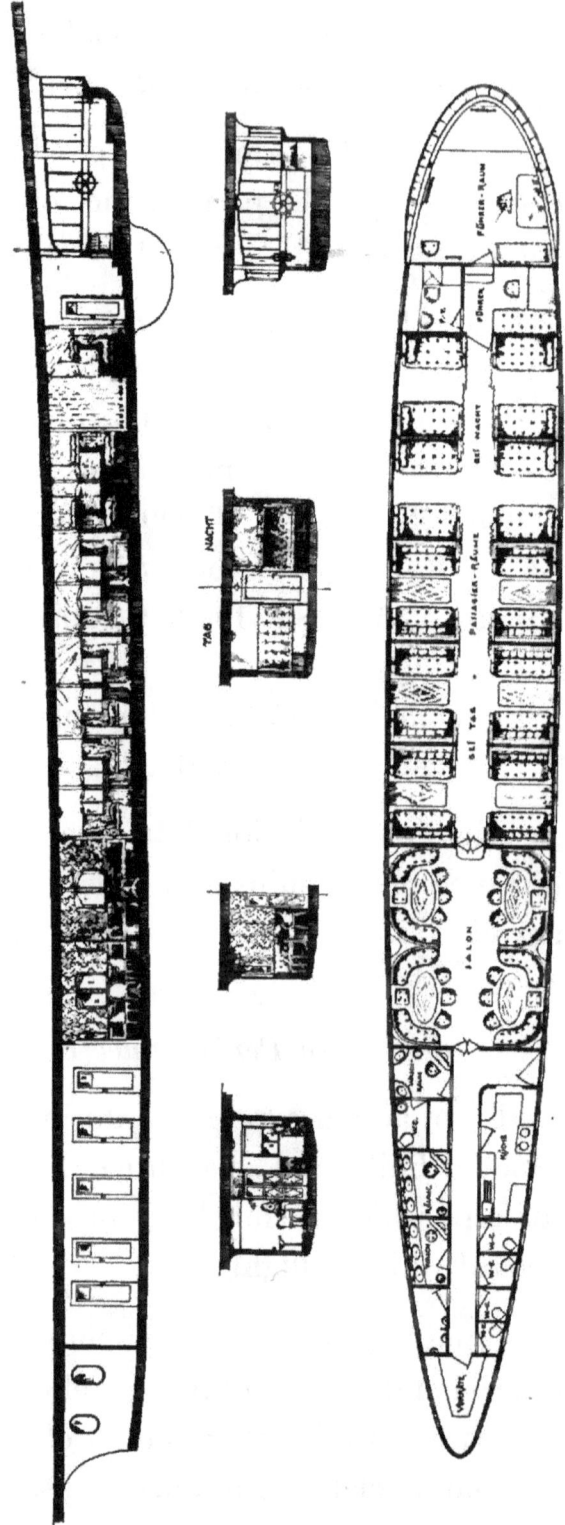

Complete Airship Navigation Data Now Available

The Zeppelin Operating Company ("DELAG") have collaborated in assembling all possible data relative to the operation and navigation of the great rigids, with a view toward having it available for immediate use and the instruction of other personnel when and wherever circumstances permit or require.

Aerial transport requirements of the future have been the subject of exhaustive study and research. Many new inventions have resulted from this knowledge of what is necessary to realize even part of the almost limitless possibilities in airship communication. Innumerable ideas have been created and passed upon by experts who have decided finally as to their practicability and financial worth.

The "DELAG," which it will be noted, is the navigating company of the Zeppelin organization, has retained all of its 1919 personnel and has added to it such forces as the outlook for the future seems to warrant. The "DELAG" has about all of the qualified airship personnel in Central Europe.

Zeppelin Organization Equipped for New Conditions

The parent company, Luftschiffbau-Zeppelin, has so arranged its organization that it can handle any development arising from the new situation both politically and economically.

Heretofore the management was under Director-General Alfred Colsman alone. Today it is divided into three divisions, operating, constructing and financial. Mr. Colsman handles the financial divisions and various subsidiary companies. Dr. Ludwig Duerr the construction, and Dr. Hugo Eckener the operating division which includes also the technical phases and all outside relations, domestic and foreign. Dr. Eckener, meanwhile, retains his position as managing Director of the "DELAG" and as one of the Directors of the Zeppelin endowment.

PLATE 56

135,000 Cubic Meter Fast Passenger Zeppelin Drawing Room.

135,000 Cubic Meter Fast Passenger Zeppelin—Stateroom.

Considered from all angles, due to the present development and knowledge of the science of lighter-than-air, it is possible today to provide satisfactory airship service for any route contemplated or which may be planned for the future.

Two and a Half Days Trans-Atlantic Service Possible

Carefully prepared calculations on some 600 flights made up and carried out from daily weather maps of the north Atlantic on methodically selected periods, have convinced the Zeppelin officials that a two and a half day Zeppelin service could be maintained between Europe and America.

Zeppelin engineers worked incessantly making the North Atlantic flights across the weather maps. When they had completed their 600 theoretical trips they knew as much about what actually could be done, as if they had flown such a service for two or three years. With the exception of a few details, easily worked out in a brief experimental period, the Zeppelin organization could put such a service in operation at once, if permitted.

New York-Chicago Route Difficult but Practicable

There has been considerable speculation relative to the New York-Chicago route. Several announcements have been made that either an airplane or airship service was about to be started. The Zeppelin engineers came to the United States not long ago and made a preliminary survey of that route. They based their report on a thorough examination of daily weather maps and reports for the last thirty years and stated that a New York-Chicago route could be operated successfully. It was pointed out that the New York-Chicago line would assume more responsibility for the fair name of commercial airship transport than anywhere on earth, more so, even than the trans-atlantic route which, technically, is far less difficult.

PLATE 57

The "DELAG" Passenger Zeppelin "Bordensee".
The new palace at Potsdam as seen enroute.

The "DELAG" Passenger Zeppelin "Bodensee."
View of Reichsteig Building and Unten den Linden, Berlin.

When asked to cooperate in a New York-Chicago airship line, the Zeppelin organization has consistently pointed out the many problems to be met. Their preliminary survey shows that they can maintain a twelve hour schedule, with almost 100% regularity in summer, from 80 to 90% in winter, or an average yearly performance of from 93 to 96%.

Many Engineering Problems Solved

In addition, the Zeppelin organization supports its conclusion with a fund of engineering data. Considerable research work has resulted in solving many problems including passenger accommodations and the structure of larger airships, improvement of the gasoline engine, the steam turbine and the Diesel engine. They have provided for the safety of gas containers, eliminating fire and lightning risk, even producing a nitrogen mantle.

Gearings, reversible propellers and modern methods of ballast recovery have been perfected or improved.

Various devices for launching ships, rotary sheds accommodating two giant Zeppelins yet revolving under light power from electric motors, and many other docking facilities are primarily of Zeppelin origin.

Zeppelin has also improved methods for fabricating all-metal commercial planes.

Zeppelin Now Aims to Increase Efficiency

Many of the problems in commercial airship operations or design will be solved shortly after actual operations are started. The aim of Zeppelin engineers has been to increase the efficiency of the airship as it has been proven that the financial returns from airship transport are, or should be, proportionately increased by the use of larger ships. The Zeppelin efforts, therefore, is to secure greater efficiency

PLATE 58

The "DELAG" Passenger Zeppelin "Bodensee."
View of Brandenburger Gate—Berlin in Winter.

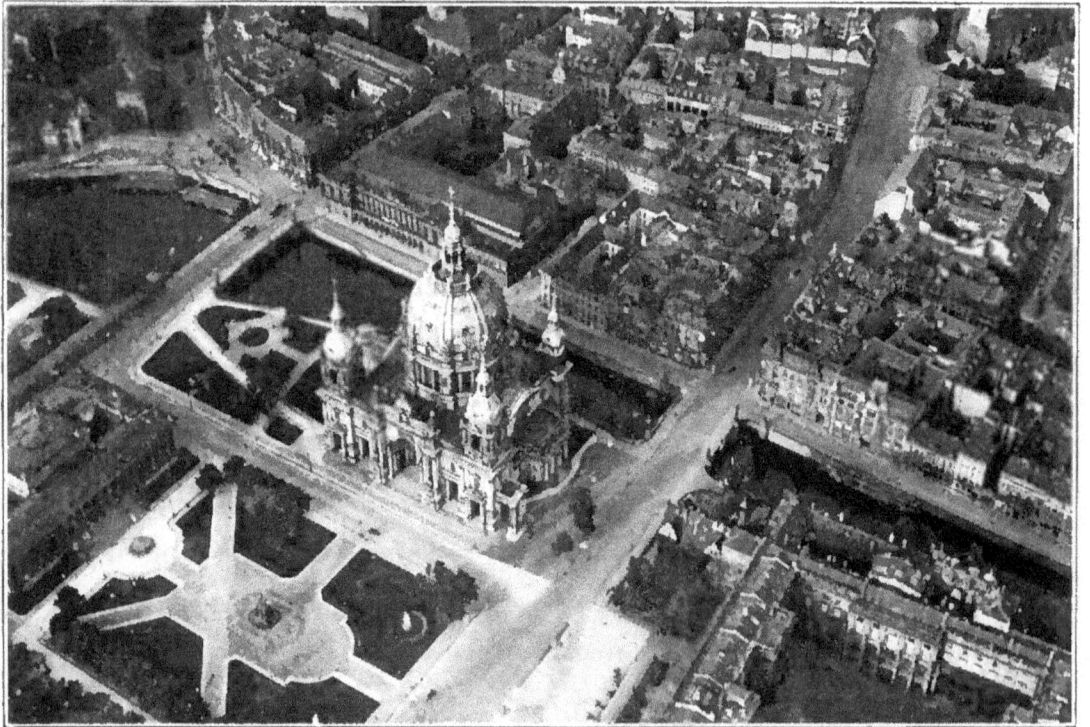

The "DELAG" Passenger Zeppelin "Bodensee."
View of Berlin in Winter.

which will allow better financial returns with smaller units and less expense.

Commercial Operations Data Compiled

While this has been one of the principal objectives of the engineering branch, the operating staffs have developed new methods of handling the big ships commercially; improved organizations, and methods and apparatus for making coast and geodetic surveys by airship, forest fire patrol, and scientific explorations.

Their investigations of weather and technical conditions have extended throughout the world; one of the principal surveys of proposed routes being between Spain and Buenos Aires, in which it was learned that a normal schedule can be maintained regularly with ninety-six hours allotted for non-stop flights between the two terminals.

The Public will Accept Airship Transportation Here as Abroad

Of course, the public must be converted to the use of the airship, just as the people of Germany were converted—by actual operations. There probably exists no other field of human endeavor so essential to our civilization as that of transportation. The traveling public has accepted other mediums of conveyance after they had demonstrated inherent qualities of safety and reliability. So it is with aircraft. Heavier-than-air machines have gradually popularized flying. Persons are riding by the air route in constantly increasing numbers, here and abroad. Their faith in commercial aviation is due solely to the BRAVE pioneering efforts of a few men of vision these last twenty years. Popularity and general use depends on the efficiency of the organizations which now carry on the work so well begun.

Zeppelin Ready to Participate in Development Throughout the World

It is the privilege of Zeppelin to participate in this development along the lines laid out by the founder, to the end that the rigid airship may do its part in bringing men and nations more closely together and facilitate mutual understanding and good will throughout the world.

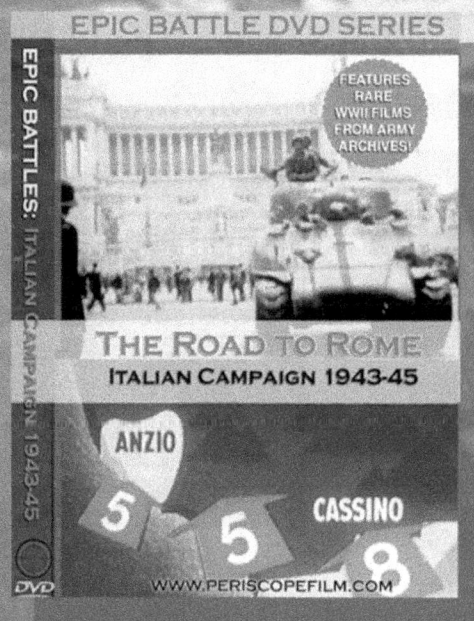

SPRUCE GOOSE

HUGHES FLYING BOAT MANUAL

RESTRICTED

Originally Published by the War Department
Reprinted by Periscope Film LLC

NOW AVAILABLE!